INTRODUCING ALICE MUNRO'S *LIVES OF GIRLS AND WOMEN*

Canadian Fiction Studies

Introducing Margaret Laurence's *The Stone Angel* CFS 1
Introducing Hugh MacLennan's *Barometer Rising* CFS 2
Introducing Margaret Atwood's *The Edible Woman* CFS 3
Introducing Margaret Atwood's *Surfacing* CFS 4
Introducing Mordecai Richler's *The Apprenticeship of Duddy Kravitz* CFS 5
Introducing Sinclair Ross's *As for Me and My House* CFS 6
Introducing Farley Mowat's *The Dog Who Wouldn't Be* CFS 7
Introducing Alice Munro's *Lives of Girls and Women* CFS 8
Introducing Timothy Findley's *The Wars* CFS 9
Introducing Hugh MacLennan's *Two Solitudes* CFS 10
Other volumes in preparation

Introducing
ALICE MUNRO'S

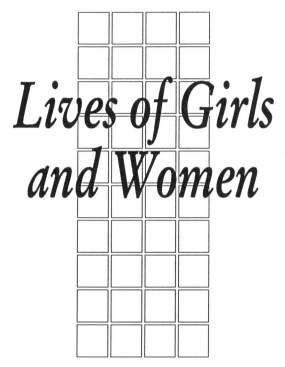

Lives of Girls and Women

A READER'S GUIDE BY
Neil K. Besner

ECW PRESS

Copyright © ECW PRESS, 1990

CANADIAN CATALOGUING IN PUBLICATION DATA

Besner, Neil Kalman, 1949–
Introducing Alice Munro's Lives of girls and women

(Canadian fiction studies ; no. 8)
Bibliography : p. 115.
Includes index.
ISBN 1-55022-122-1

1. Munro, Alice, 1931–   . Lives of girls and women.
I. Title. II. Series.

PS8576.U57L583 1990   C813'.54   C89-095002-4
PR9199.3.M8L583 1990

This book has been published with the assistance of grants
from The Canada Council, the Ontario Arts Council, and
the Government of Canada Department of Communications.

The cover features a reproduction of the dust-wrapper from
the first edition of *Lives of Girls and Women*, courtesy of the
Thomas Fisher Rare Book Library, University of Toronto.
Frontispiece photograph by R.J. Nephew
Photography, Goderich, Ontario.
Design and imaging by ECW Type & Art, Oakville, Ontario.
Printed by University of Toronto Press, North York, Ontario.

Distributed by Butterworths Canada Ltd.
75 Clegg Road, Markham, Ontario L6G 1A1

Published by ECW PRESS
307 Coxwell Avenue, Toronto, Ontario M4L 3B5

Table of Contents

A Note on the Author	6
Chronology	9
The Importance of the Work	12
Critical Reception	16
Reading of the Text	32
Form: The Novel and Its Stories	32
"The Flats Road": Uncle Benny and Stories of Family	35
"Heirs of the Living Body": The Death of a History	42
"Princess Ida": A Mother's Stories Retold	50
"Age of Faith": What If God Were Real?	62
"Changes and Ceremonies": The Operetta of Love	69
"Lives of Girls and Women": A Phallic Story Untold	78
"Baptizing": Wordless Love and Real Life	89
"Epilogue: The Photographer": How Del Writes	103
Epilogue: The Reader, the Text, and the Real	112
Works Cited	115
Index	121

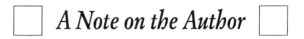

A Note on the Author

Neil K. Besner is Associate Professor of English at the University of Winnipeg. His critical study, *The Light of Imagination: Mavis Gallant's Fiction*, appeared in 1988. His other publications include articles on Commonwealth writers and on composition theory, and biocritical entries and reviews on Canadian, American, and Latin American books and writers. He is currently co-editing an anthology of modern English short fiction.

NOTE ON THE TEXT

The most widely available edition of *Lives of Girls and Women* is the Signet/New American Library paperback text, first reprinted from the McGraw-Hill hardcover edition (1971) in 1974. Readers should be warned that the Signet text has many errors, the most obvious of which is the title of the first section, misprinted as "The Flat Roads" at the top of every page (1–23), and subsequently misprinted both on the Table of Contents page and at the head of every page in the reprint of the Signet edition. Interestingly, the second Signet reprint, unlike the first, describes the book as "nonfiction" on its spine — an inadvertent acknowledgement from the publisher, perhaps, of the persistent desire to read this book as autobiography.

ACKNOWLEDGEMENTS

I would like to thank Leslie Gentes, who provided invaluable research assistance at many stages. Apollonia Steele in the Special Collections Division of the University of Calgary Library was most helpful in guiding me through the Alice Munro papers collected there, and Jean Moore kindly gave me permission to reproduce much of the information she had compiled in "An Alice Munro Chronology," published in the second Accession Guide to the Alice Munro Papers. My students in Canadian literature classes at Mount Royal College in Calgary and at the University of Winnipeg endured my questions and responded to *Lives of Girls and Women* in ways that challenged many of my assumptions; I owe them, individually and collectively, a large debt and much gratitude. I would like to thank Alice Munro, who was kind and prompt in her responses to my questions and requests. And first and last, I owe thanks to my wife Carlene, who remains my most faithful critic, and to my children Daniel and Barbara for their patience.

Introducing
Alice Munro's
Lives of Girls and Women

Chronology

1931	Alice Laidlaw is born 10 July in Wingham, Ontario, to Robert Eric Laidlaw and Anne Clarke Chamney Laidlaw.
1949–51	Attends the University of Western Ontario on a scholarship.
1950	First published short story: "The Dimensions of a Shadow" in *Folio* (University of Western Ontario), April 1950.
1951	Sells first story, "The Strangers," to Robert Weaver for the Canadian Broadcasting Corporation; marries James A. Munro.
1952	Moves to Vancouver, B.C., and works for three years for the Vancouver Public Library.
1953	Daughter Sheila is born on 5 October.
1953	Publishes "A Basket of Strawberries" in *Mayfair*, November 1953, the first of many stories published over the next twenty-five years in Canadian and American periodicals such as *Canadian Forum*, *Chatelaine*, *Montrealer*, *Queen's Quarterly*, *Tamarack Review*, and *The New Yorker*. Stories are also read over CBC and several are adapted for television.
1955	Daughter Catherine is born 28 July; dies 29 July.
1957	Daughter Jenny is born on 4 June.
1963	Moves to Victoria, B.C., where she and her husband establish Munro's Books, which is still running and successful.
1966	Daughter Andrea is born on 8 September.
1968	First book of stories, *Dance of the Happy Shades*, is published and wins Governor-General's Award for Fiction.

1971	*Lives of Girls and Women* is published and wins Canadian Booksellers Award.
1972	Wins B.C. Library Association Outstanding Fiction Writer's Award; moves back to Ontario.
1973	Teaches at Notre Dame University, Nelson, B.C., during summer.
1974	Book of stories, *Something I've Been Meaning to Tell You*, is published; *Dance of the Happy Shades* wins Great Lakes Colleges Association New Writer Award.
1974–75	Writer-in-Residence at the University of Western Ontario.
1976	Awarded an honourary doctorate from the University of Western Ontario.
1976	Marries Gerald Fremlin.
1977	First recipient of Canada-Australia Literary Prize.
1978	Book of linked stories, *Who Do You Think You Are?* (published in the U.S. in 1979 and the U.K. in 1980 as *The Beggar Maid*) wins Governor-General's Award for Fiction. Writes screenplay for "1847: The Irish," telecast by CBC as part of the series *The Newcomers/Les Arrivants*.
1979	Travels to Australia as part of the award for the 1977 Canada-Australia Literary Prize.
1980	Writer-in-Residence from January to April at the University of British Columbia and September-October at the University of Queensland, Australia.
1980	Cited by the Foundation for the Advancement of Canadian Letters, and wins Periodical Distributors of Canada Award for the Canadian Paperback edition of *Who Do You Think You Are?*
1980	Short-listed for the Booker Prize for Fiction for *The Beggar Maid*.
1981	Travels to China with several other Canadian writers, as recorded in *Chinada: Memoirs of The Gang of Seven*, ed. Gary Geddes (1982).
1981	The Alice Munro Papers are presented to the University of Calgary.
1982	*The Moons of Jupiter*, a book of stories, is published.

	Munro travels to Norway, Sweden, and Denmark in connection with the Norwegian translation of *The Beggar Maid*, *Tiggerpiken*.
1982	Conference on Alice Munro's work held at the University of Waterloo, Waterloo, Ontario, and papers published as *The Art of Alice Munro: Saying the Unsayable*, ed. Judith Miller (1984).
1984	Atlantis Films wins Oscar in live-action short category for adaptation of "Boys and Girls," a story collected in *Dance of the Happy Shades*.
1986	*The Progress of Love*, a book of stories, is published and wins Governor-General's Award for Fiction. Munro becomes the first recipient of the Marian Engel Award.
1990	*Friend of My Youth*, a book of stories, is published.

The Importance of the Work

Over the last twenty years, the short story in English has grown out of its traditional role in the family of fiction as a promising daughter, or at best an attractive little sister, to the novel. It is more difficult for us now than it ever was to think of the short story in such patronizing terms — to see it as a training ground, an apprenticeship for novelists on their way to mastering the major form. In Canada, we can see the contemporary rise of the short story reflected on a practical level simply in the disproportionately large number of our best writers who work mainly, sometimes almost exclusively, in the short story form. By wide agreement in the English-speaking world, Alice Munro is one of the finest of our contemporary writers. On the evidence of her work to date — some eighty stories published over the last twenty-five years, most of them collected in six books, three of which have won Governor-General's Awards for Fiction — Munro's preference clearly has been for the short story, and she herself has much to say about the reasons for her attraction to the form.

And yet the form and the mode of Munro's second book, *Lives of Girls and Women* — a book that has attracted continuing critical attention since its publication in 1971 — have long been a matter for debate. In bibliographies of Munro's work, it is always referred to as a novel. Munro herself refers to it as a novel in a prefatory disclaimer that has raised other questions: "This novel is autobiographical in form but not in fact. My family, neighbors and friends did not serve as models." Connections between autobiography and fiction have fascinated some of Munro's readers; like many other Canadian writers, Munro has pointed out that we tend to assume all too eagerly that fiction *is* autobiography, that the setting of Jubilee in *Lives of Girls and Women*, for example, *is* Wingham, Ontario, where Munro grew up, or that many of the characters so clearly depicted by the book's protagonist, Del Jordan — Del's mother and father, her brother Owen, her "Uncle" Benny, her friend Naomi, or her lover, Garnet French — *are* the actual people that Alice Munro grew up with in Wingham.[1]

Readers have been intrigued with Munro's note: how can a novel be autobiographical in "form" but not in "fact"? And how are we to understand the subtle and pervasive interplay in this work between sets of apparently different forms, aims and conventions? The texture of *Lives of Girls and Women* presents us, as does so much of Munro's fiction, with a composition of seemingly opposed impulses organized around the documentary, objective recording of a "real" past and the imaginative recreation of a fictional one. The related tensions between realism and heightened realism, between memory's recall and imagination's artful reshaping of recollection, between the depiction of richly detailed but flat and familiar surfaces and the mysterious depths that they are shown to conceal — these inform Del Jordan's narration and articulate the range of her developing imagination.

Discussion about the form of *Lives of Girls and Women* as a novel or book of stories has usually begun by considering the connections between its parts. None of them — whether we think of them as chapters or self-contained stories — was published separately before the book appeared; and for much of the time, the chapters could stand alone as separate stories, although there are many obvious connections between them through setting, character, and chronology. Approaching the book through its several related forms — chapters in a novel, self-contained stories, and linked stories — offers readers further insight into the rhythms of Del Jordan's development.

But all consideration of the form, mode, and style of *Lives of Girls and Women* has arisen from the international recognition of the book's accomplishments. Simply put, *Lives of Girls and Women* is the most powerful and manifold exploration in contemporary Canadian writing of the development of a young girl's life, her imagination, and her imaginative life. This is why the book has gained such a wide readership in Canada and the English-speaking world at large. It is also one of many recent works that has attracted particular critical attention from feminists, who see in Munro's depiction of Del Jordan's growing awareness of the complexities of her relationships within her family and with boys and men, and of her own developing consciousness, a strong and accurate representation of contemporary girls' and women's lives. Munro herself has not always been comfortable with what she sees as an uncritical politicization and misreading of the book in these terms: Del Jordan's mother's assertion that "There is a change coming I think in the lives of girls and women," for example, has sometimes been hailed as an unequivocal truth, a self-evident affirmation, whereas Addie Morrison is shown throughout the book to be a complex character given to highly charged pronouncements that affect Del in ironic and ambiguous ways as often as not.[2]

Munro's writing is often celebrated as well for its exacting creation of a tangible sense of place. *Lives of Girls and Women* presents us with one of the fullest and most powerful evocations of the small town setting that so often figures to various regional ends in contemporary Canadian literature. Described in alternately sharp, stark, and rich detail, the streets, the weatherworn houses, and the changing seasons in Jubilee and the surrounding countryside intimately reflect the local, social and natural, psychological and imaginative forces that shape Del's developing consciousness.

To date, *Lives of Girls and Women* is also the finest Canadian book to translate the structure of the *künstlerroman* — the traditional story of the growth of a young, usually male, usually middle-class character into an artist — into female terms. (The Canadian work with which Munro's book is most often compared on this count is Margaret Laurence's highly regarded book of linked stories, *A Bird in the House* (1970), which in somewhat different ways traces the growth of another first-person narrator, Vanessa MacLeod.) *Lives of Girls and Women* is justly celebrated for Del Jordan's account of her growing awareness of herself as a writer, and has been compared in this sense with Joyce's *A Portrait of the Artist as a Young Man*. It is a story narrated in Del Jordan's voice, so that we read and hear the subjective and individual nature of the experience Del is remembering and recreating. The book has proved compelling to several generations of readers because it renders such a full and frank depiction of Del's growth as she explores and defines her relationships within her family, her apprehensions of mortality and the nature of faith, her emerging sexuality, and always, the nature of her own imagination as she discovers how language means to her, how words shape her vision and lead to her vocation as a writer of fiction.

The narrative voice and perspective Munro creates for Del are among the book's finest artistic achievements. As Del ranges over her past from childhood to young adulthood, the alternating cadences of her voice and her vocabulary, like the alternating breadth and depth of her vision, make her most remote experiences seem immediate and at the same time, allow her to detach herself from immediate experiences to describe them and speculate on their significance. Through this narrative perspective, we learn as Del learns, how she learns, and what she learns about her life, so that the reading experience seems to affirm the appropriateness of Munro's first title for the book, later discarded, but kept as the last phrase of "Baptizing": *Real Life*. "Real life," as conveyed so richly through Del Jordan's imagination, is what *Lives of Girls and Women* sets out before us so artfully, so artlessly, that we would like to believe its fiction as if it were not fact, but another kind of reality. And that is the inimitable mark of a real work of art.

Critical Reception

Looking back from 1990, we can see how the path of nineteen years of commentary on *Lives of Girls and Women* has both led and followed the general directions Canadian criticism has taken since the late sixties and early seventies. This has been a period in which Canadian fiction has gained a much wider audience at home and abroad, in English and in translation, and a period in which Canadian critics, like their American and British counterparts, have responded to several major shifts in critical theory. In the late sixties and early seventies, influenced by the linguistics of Ferdinand de Saussure, the anthropological theories of Claude Lévi-Strauss, and by Jacques Derrida's elaboration of his conception of "différance," contemporary Anglo-American literary criticism renewed its attention to the functions of language as a relational system, both in literary and non-literary texts, and to how language signifies. The major thrusts of this critical attitude produced the structuralist, poststructuralist, and deconstructive movements. In Canada, these shifts have been most noticeable in our departures from broadly thematic criticism, with its primary emphasis on defining what a literary text is "about" — what meanings literature communicates — towards a closer consideration of *how* literature conveys meaning through language, narration, form, and style. In a formulation that has now been overused so badly that it has become a cliché, critical attention has shifted from product to process, from a focus on the finite meaning of a text to a more pluralistic study of the myriad ways in which literary texts, like all texts, organize or fragment their meanings. Along with these shifts in emphasis has come, necessarily, renewed attention to precisely *how* — rather than simply *if* — the broadly accepted conventions of realism might be operating in works like *Lives of Girls and Women* to evoke fictional worlds that seem as substantively real as the world we inhabit beyond or through the text.

The other major shift in approach during this period has been the rise of feminist criticism, which has not only extended and developed structuralist theory, but has also established its own theoretical frameworks, with its own methodologies and goals. Much feminist theory begins with the fundamental assumption that accounts of women's actual experience have been suppressed, marginalized, distorted, or denied by patriarchal visions and constructions of reality — not the least of which has been the language of patriarchy, which is understood to operate in the world as it does in literary texts to deny women their voices. With its telling analyses of the power relationships between genders, its close study of the ways in which women's stories are at once concealed and revealed, suppressed and exposed in literature, and its sharp focus on the serious play conveyed through the ambiguities of language, feminist criticism has begun to radically alter and enrich our reading of writers like Munro.

In Canada, both of these developments have traced their lines of inquiry within the history of our own distinctive cultural preoccupations. Reflecting our perennial national impulse to catalogue and define our experience as means to establishing a seemingly elusive identity, our dominant critical texts in the late sixties and early seventies tended to be surveys, many of which mentioned Munro, who had won the Governor-General's Award for Fiction in 1968 with her first collection of stories, *Dance of the Happy Shades*. Munro's early stories and their settings in rural Ontario are noted by Hugo McPherson in what remains the most important and comprehensive of these works, *The Literary History of Canada: Canadian Literature in English* (1965: 720, 722); in the second edition of this work (1976: III: 270–71), William New discusses *Dance of the Happy Shades* and *Lives of Girls and Women*, and in the third edition, scheduled to appear shortly, Munro's place in contemporary writing will doubtless be discussed at greater length. Margaret Atwood comments at several points on Munro's first two books in her engaging and controversial survey, *Survival: A Thematic Guide to Canadian Literature*, including Del Jordan in her chapter on "The Paralyzed Artist" (1972: 193); Frank Davey includes Munro in *From There to Here: A Guide to English-Canadian Literature Since 1960* (1974: 201–04). Elizabeth Waterston cites Munro in her *Survey: A Short History of Canadian Literature* (1973: 72–3, 167, 207, 208), and

Norah Story includes an entry on Munro in *Supplement to the Oxford Companion to Canadian History and Literature* (1973: 235). In a more extended form, John Moss considers Munro's fiction in "Alice in the Looking Glass: *Lives of Girls and Women*" in his book *Sex and Violence in the Canadian Novel: The Ancestral Present* (1977: 54–68). This impulse to map the general contours of our literature remains, as seen in the two editions of John Moss's *A Reader's Guide to the Canadian Novel* (1981: 215–17; 1987: 276–79) or in Charles Steele's edition recording a 1978 discussion of our fiction, *Taking Stock: The Calgary Conference on the Canadian Novel* (1982), in which *Lives of Girls and Women* placed very well in that conference's controversial — some would say notoriously Canadian — ballot to select the most important Canadian novels (151). W.J. Keith discusses Munro in his literary survey, *Canadian Literature in English* (1985), as does Linda Hutcheon in her study, *The Canadian Postmodern: A Survey of Contemporary English-Canadian Fiction* (1988). The most recent and most comprehensive of these texts — William New's *A History of Canadian Literature* (1989) — refers to Munro's fiction in several contexts.

Complementing and developing the maps of Canadian literature drawn in our surveys, a steadily increasing number of articles in periodicals began to focus more specifically on individual Canadian writers, on individual texts, and on individual aspects of writers' works. This closer study of particular texts has coincided roughly with the rise of periodicals devoted exclusively to the study of Canadian literature; it was only thirty-one years ago, twelve years before the publication of *Lives of Girls and Women*, that *Canadian Literature*, the first such journal, was established by George Woodcock at the University of British Columbia, and full courses in Canadian literature in our colleges and universities became more common only in the 1960s.

Before turning to the commentary on *Lives of Girls and Women* in more detail, one other major development is worth noting: the rise of the short story. For reasons that no one has fully explained to date — and in the face of the longstanding preference for the novel form, by publishers and readers alike — a significant number of our finest contemporary writers often turn to the short story as their chosen form. The progress of Munro's career can now be seen as having not simply coincided with, but more accurately as also having precipitated the ascendance of the Canadian short story in its many contemporary forms. In the same issue of *Canadian Literature* that published one of the first, and also the most perceptive review of *Lives of Girls and Women*, by James Polk, Donald Stephens remarks in "The Bright New Day," a review article discussing five books of stories, that the Canadian short story "did, through writers like Wilson, Callaghan, and Gallant, achieve for Canadian literature an international reputation, before very many of our poets and novelists became known abroad" (84). Stephens notes that an entire recent issue of *World Literature Written in English* (April 1972) focuses exclusively on the Canadian short story, evidence of the increased attention criticism was paying to the form. In Canada, Munro, along with Mavis Gallant, is now generally placed at the head of the group of writers who work almost exclusively in the short story form. But a preliminary list of our better known writers who often turn to the short story — writers from a wide range of regions, depicting an equally wide range of settings, and writing in widely different voices, styles, and forms — might begin on the west coast and end in the east with Audrey Thomas, Jack Hodgins, Jane Rule, Leon Rooke, Keath Fraser, George Bowering, Rudy Wiebe, Guy Vanderhaeghe, Sandra Birdsell, Carol Shields, Margaret Laurence, Timothy Findley, Marian Engel, Norman Levine, Matt Cohen, Isabel Huggan, Margaret Atwood, Hugh Hood, John Metcalf, Janice Kulyk Keefer, David Adams Richards, and Alistair MacLeod. To indulge in speculation for a moment, this turn to the short story form and to related forms like the novella, the book of linked stories, and the novel that is composed of seemingly self-contained episodes may be a sign of a related perceptual shift — or, to borrow another overused term from the social sciences, a paradigm shift — reflected in Canadian writing as well as in writing from other cultures and languages. Perhaps many contemporary writers are finding that these less monolithically unified, more fragmented forms, traditionally more sharply focused on the significance of intense but isolated moments, of sudden but fleeting insights, or on the half-promise of vital revelations, might be forms better suited than the novel to reflect the radical discontinuities of our contemporary experience.

Regardless of the causes or significance of the rise of the form, it is clear that it continues to compel readers, writers, and scholars; the critical attention currently being paid internationally to the short story is only one measure of the extent of this development. Canadian literature in general and the short story in particular have recently been the focus of widespread critical discussion in Europe. In the last five years, there have been two conferences on the Canadian short story in English in Strasbourg, France, with a third planned for 1990, and there was an international conference on the short story in Paris in 1988. Several critical journals are devoted exclusively to studies of the form, and the proceedings of the Strasbourg conferences, which include substantial discussion of Munro's work, were published in special issues of *RANAM* (Recherches Anglaises et Nord-Americaines). At home, the first and second editions of the *Canadian Encyclopedia* include entries by J.R. (Tim) Struthers, "Short Fiction in English" (1985, III: 1692–93; 1988, III: 1996–97) as do standard texts like *The Oxford Companion to Canadian Literature*, which includes Robert Weaver's entry, "Short Stories in English" (752–56).

REVIEWS

The first reviews of a work often initiate the critical discussion that develops around it, and the commentary that has animated our reading of *Lives of Girls and Women* typifies this pattern.[3] Reflecting the perception of Canadian writing that was still current in the United States and Britain, early reviews from these countries praised the book as a highly accomplished, but still as a somewhat exotically regional, somewhat unexpected success. And reviewers abroad and in Canada alike began the still unresolved debate over the book's form and its connections with autobiography. The flavour of the opening paragraph of Christopher Wordsworth's "Maple Leaf in Bud" in *The Manchester Guardian Weekly* provides a pungent illustration of several of these qualities:

> Canada, not a great seed-bed of the arts, has found a considerable talent in Alice Munro. *Lives of Girls and Women* has the core and growth of a good novel and, though episodic in a way that shows its author's apprenticeship to the short-story form, is held together by living tissue. To describe it as a clever and receptive girl's progress through childhood to adolescent experience may

not sound very mouth-watering, since every week has its quota on that theme. The setting — a fox farm in the muskeg swamps of Ontario with a neighbouring township where the spirit of its Scots Presbyterian founders broods disapprovingly — gives it the fillip of unfamiliarity; sensitive and tensile writing lends strength as well as charm. (24)

The rhetorical question, revealing in itself, that opens Marigold Johnson's review in the *New Statesman* is never quite answered, and she is one of many to cite the book's allegedly comical treatment of women's liberation through its portrait of Del's mother, to read the work as autobiography, and to confuse Alice Munro with Del Jordan as the narrator of the work:

> Are we still condescending philistines towards contemporary Commonwealth literature? *Lives of Girls and Women,* by a new Canadian prizewinner, belongs securely in its small town of Jubilee on the Wawanash River, where the Gay-la Dance Hall with its chocolate-coloured imitation log walls is denounced as Sodom, where they cram the Town Hall for *The Gypsy Princess,* and where the garbage collector, Pork Childs, owns peacocks. On the last page Alice Munro steps outside her adolescent narrator, Del, to lament that no memorialised topography can do Jubilee justice . . . . Yet, episodic and sometimes repetitive as this scrapbook of anecdotes appears, this is more than local nostalgia — and much funnier, especially on the women's liberation front . . . . Alice Munro writes with an unselfconscious immediacy and intelligence that one hopes will range outside these highly enjoyable autobiographical sketches. (619)

Geoffrey Wolff's review in *Time* is more enthusiastic, tempered as it might be on one hand by his chaste assessment that Munro's "achievement is small but fine" and on the other by his exultant closing, "Call it fiction: praise it." But his opening comments also qualify his high praise:

> Despite this young Canadian's conventional disclaimer that her novel is "autobiographical in form but not in fact," the pleasure to be taken from it comes from its fidelity to things as we imagine they really were. The book is a fiction for people who like to read brittle, yellow clips from newspapers published in towns

where they never lived, who like to look through the snapshot albums of imperfect strangers. (66).

The most perceptive British review, by Patricia Beers in the *Times Literary Supplement*, notes that the novel "more closely resembles a series of short stories," but then contrasts it with an unlikely and lurid American counterpart, Lisa Alther's *Kinflicks*, and with a homegrown pastoral/sentimental school of writing: "Neither does it fall flat into the long, lush grass of so many British autobiographies and novels about country adolescence. It is an honest book" (302).

Generally, the book fared better in Canadian reviews. Writing in the *University of Toronto Quarterly* in 1972, O.H.T. Rudzik remarks in his overview of the year's fiction that Munro's book contains a "subtly and palpably defined county of the sensibility..." (313–14). Rudzik reads it as "an accumulation of a life evolved in that finely mythical past of a small southwestern Ontario town. Liberation from it involves understanding something that must be recaptured and cannibalized, and repeated" (314). Jane Rule's review in *Books in Canada* is both warm and insightful; Rule is the first to note what subsequent criticism has elaborated — that "Among other things, *Lives of Girls and Women* is a portrait of the artist as a young girl who is stripped of nothing she cannot better do without and given all that she needs to go on" (5). Reviewing for the *Canadian Forum*, Heather Jackson opens by asserting what many other reviewers hint at:

> Perhaps the first thing to say about Alice Munro's novel *Lives of Girls and Women* is that it is not a novel. This is not just carping: it seems to me to be such a good collection of short stories that is [sic] would be a mistake to pretend it is anything else. However, for those who like a novel, it must be admitted that all the stories in *Lives* are set in one place, the small Ontario town which is the context of one girl's life, and that they deal with some of the conventional crises — intellectual and social as well as physical — of growing up. (76)

In a more wide ranging, and also more provocative review in the *Journal of Canadian Fiction*, Clara Thomas suggests that *Lives* can be read within the rich tradition in Canadian literature of "autobiographical and fictional accounts of female adolescence," although "each work has its own uniqueness." At first, the most surprising of Thomas's assertions, but one that she goes on to qualify, concerns Del Jordan's fictional lineage:

> Alice Munro's fictional heroine, Del Jordan, has more in common with L.M. Montgomery's Anne than does any other central figure of one of these books — and I mean that as a compliment to both Mrs. Munro and L.M. Montgomery. Anne's appeal — her archetypal appeal if you will — rests in the invincibility of her spirit and its triumph. Against all odds and opponents Anne remains joyously herself and it is this confirmation of every female's heart's desire which explains her staying-power through generations of young readers.... The same is true of Del Jordan. Experience neither conquers nor changes her essential selfhood. (95)

Although Thomas finds it difficult to believe that Del can remain unscarred by her experiences, she recognizes that Del incarnates many contemporary women's strongest hopes:

> I am not at all sure that it is humanly and psychologically possible to grow up as unaffected by fear, guilt or anxiety as Del Jordan seems to be. But I am perfectly certain that her powerful and unconquerable will towards psychic survival and autonomy is shared by all of us at least some of the time, and that for most women between eighteen and eighty she must emanate an astonishing and sometimes a terrifying authenticity. (95)

Thomas is also one of the first readers to note the problem that the last section of the book, "Epilogue: The Photographer" presents. Munro has often commented on how difficult this section was to write and yet how necessary she felt it to be;[4] Thomas reads this section, not as "an addendum, written to paste a narrative cement" but as a "containment of statements of purpose and effect" (96).

The most comprehensive and insightful review of *Lives and Girls and Women*, "Deep Caves and Kitchen Linoleum" (a phrase destined to become the most often quoted from this book) appeared in the autumn 1972 issue of *Canadian Literature*. Without sacrificing seriousness or scope, James Polk's discussion is incisive, instructive, and written with a flair and style all too rare in our reviews or more extended critical commentary. Polk opens by showing how the novel is "conventional to a fault," but goes on to distinguish it from its British and American kin and from its closer Canadian relations, and to point to Munro's distinctive treatment of her small town setting:

> Alice Munro's first novel is about a sensitive young girl growing up in a small Ontario town in the 1940's. To say as much is to summon up the arthritic ghosts of a thousand other first novels from library vault and desk drawer, and to suggest the kind of risk an author takes writing a conventional village bildungsroman in this age of pop, camp, funk, porno, and junk.... This is the universal pattern for a first novel, although the British might require more misery at public school, the French more adultery, the Americans more violence.... [Munro's] class bias is unusual when one considers how often Ontario small towns are shaped into those safe, bourgeois organisms sustaining clergymen, lawyers and young lovers, just right for slightly academic comedies of manners (Robertson Davies, Stephen Leacock) or lyrical-gothic allegory (James Reaney). In Munro's work we see Ontario social myths from the bottom up; the poverty line runs smack through her part of town and her characters seem curiously estranged from their environment: the men struggle in silence to earn a living, the women — Munro's particular concern — are shown to be troubled by isolation and unfulfilled dreams. (102)

Like Thomas, Polk sees the epilogue as "undoubtedly a statement of the author's own artistic purposes," although he goes on to suggest it defines "the fictional realist ... as a not-quite-demonic photographer who strives to reveal important truths through pictures of 'ordinary' surfaces" (103). But Polk is more troubled than Thomas by this section, seeing it as "an advertisement for the writer's abilities rather than an afterword organically connected to the novel itself" (103). This discomfort leads to Polk's major reservation about the book, one that figures as an important starting point in the ongoing debate about the book's form. He finds that the novel's shape is a "loosely-woven, anecdotal structure, in which the chapters, basically unpruned short stories, are casually linked together by Del's consciousness ..." (104). Comparing this book to *Dance of the Happy*

Shades, Polk remarks that although "both the novel and the stories are funny, well-written, and evocative, it seems that the novel misses out on that black, brutal cutting edge that gives the stories their idiosyncratic power" (104).

I have quoted at length from Polk's review and from others because they anticipate so many of the critical debates that followed them — debates about the book's form, its realism, its narration and point of view, its presentation of girls' and women's experience, and its evocation of Del Jordan. The critical commentary that began to appear hard on the heels of the early reviews deepened and widened the discussions that continue to engage us twenty years later, and will not be resolved very soon.

CRITICISM

The sheer volume of critical articles on *Lives of Girls and Women* makes it impossible to list or discuss them all here, or to do much more than cite the five books and two collections of essays on Munro's work that have appeared to date.[5] Much of the bibliographical work has already been done in several places: Robert Thacker's "Alice Munro: An Annotated Bibliography" (1984: 5: 354–414) is the most complete compilation.[6] But J.R. (Tim) Struthers has evidence that the mass of commentary on Munro's work appears to have inhibited some of Munro's critics: in a bibliography of criticism on Munro's works compiled for *Studies in Canadian Literature* three years earlier than Thacker's bibliography, Struthers observes that although he found more than eighty articles or parts of books that discuss Munro's work, it was "somewhat shocking to discover that only *three* articles quote or comment on the work of other critics" (140). In addition to these two bibliographies, there are several others that cite more recent criticism, particularly the listings at the ends of the two most recent books on Munro, W.R. Martin's *Alice Munro: Paradox and Parallel* (1987) and E.D. Blodgett's *Alice Munro* (1988), in which Blodgett annotates the articles he cites.

Given this wealth of bibliographical information, I have chosen to trace the major directions of this growing body of criticism, and to identify one or two representative studies in each area.

INITIATION, *BILDUNGSROMAN*, AND *KÜNSTLERROMAN*

As we saw with early reviews of *Lives of Girls and Women*, many readers have traced the path of Del Jordan's development from childhood through adolescence *and* as an emerging artist. Critical studies developing this approach include a discussion by J.R. (Tim) Struthers, "Reality and Ordering: The Growth of a Young Artist in *Lives of Girls and Women*," in which he shows the influence of James Joyce's *A Portrait of the Artist as a Young Man* and *Ulysses* on Munro's work. The influence of Joyce is also pursued by W. R. Martin in "Alice Munro and James Joyce." Studies of Del's development in more general terms include Miriam Packer's "*Lives of Girls and Women*: A Creative Search for Completion," and, more recently, Lorraine M. York's comparative study, "Lives of Joan and Del: Separate Paths to Transformation in *Lives of Girls and Women* and *Lady Oracle*."

PARADOX, PARALLEL, AND DOUBLE VISION

Early in its development, Munro criticism began to note the several kinds of oppositions that seemed to be operating in her fiction. These included oppositions between words — between adjectives and nouns, for example, or between pairs of adjectives; between individual characters' contradictory attitudes, narrators' contradictory descriptions of their experience, of reactions to events, of impressions of time — generally, oppositions between and within many of the interpretive and narrative acts of Munro's characters. This line of inquiry includes explorations of sets of oppositions between the resources of memory that yield an apparently "true" documentary realism, and the resources of invention and imagination that yield recreations that underline their own status as fictions shaped to reveal their own ambiguous truths. The discussions that speak most directly to these sets of contradictions include Helen Hoy's article, " 'Dull, Simple, Amazing and Unfathomable': Paradox and Double Vision in Alice Munro's Fiction." Hoy takes her title from Del Jordan's closing observation about the contradictory truths about people's lives, "in Jubilee as elsewhere" (210). Hoy's close analysis of the ways in which oxymorons work in Munro's language provides the basis for her exploration of Munro's "double vision," through which, as many other critics have suggested, conflicts are rarely resolved, and social and psychological realities are most often revealed to be at least double-edged, if not many layered or paradoxical. The major strength of Hoy's discussion is that it works outward to its conception of Munro's vision from a closely detailed study of the language of Munro's fiction, showing how descriptions that incarnate contradiction — "heartless applause," "smiling angrily," "hungry laughter," "tender pain," "tolerant outrage" (104), for example — provide the particular ground for Munro's vision of reality, so that in *Lives of Girls and Women*,

> Munro is doing more ... than simply identifying differences in life-styles. These visions, internally coherent and explicitly identified as independent worlds, in most cases vie with each other for the exclusive right to define experience. In the end none has ultimate authority; each is clearly presented as *one* reality in the context of others. (110)

This line of discussion is pursued in several related ways by Munro's critics, most fully, perhaps, by W.R. Martin in "The Strange and the Familiar in Alice Munro" and in his book *Alice Munro: Paradox and Parallel.*

REGIONALISM

Drawing on her work and on what Munro has said in interviews about the influence of writers like Eudora Welty — in particular, of Welty's *The Golden Apples* — and of other writers from the American south, several of Munro's critics have shown how these regional influences inform Munro's exploration of southwestern Ontario. Among these studies are a discussion by J.R. (Tim) Struthers, "Alice Munro and the American South," Nora Robson's study, "Alice Munro and the White American South: The Quest," and Sandra Djwa's "Deep Caves and Kitchen Linoleum: Psychological Violence in the Fiction of Alice Munro."

NARRATION

In *Lives of Girls and Women* as in most of Munro's fiction, the control of narration and point of view is crucial because Munro's narrators so often create a complex weave of the past recollected and reported, and the past as it shapes and inhabits the present. Many critics have studied this central element in Munro's art; representative discussions include Robert Thacker's " 'Clear Jelly': Alice Munro's Narrative Dialectics," John Orange's "Alice Munro and a Maze of Time," Susan Warwick's study of retrospective narration in *Lives* and *Who Do You Think You Are?*, "Growing Up: The Novels of Alice Munro," and most recently, the valuable commentary by E.D. Blodgett in *Alice Munro* on "focalization" (10–12), the term he uses to define more closely the ways in which he studies narration in Munro's fiction.

AUTOBIOGRAPHICAL FICTION

The issues of autobiographical form and intention have been debated since early reviewers noted Munro's prefatory disclaimer about the book. In keeping with the attention recent critical theory has paid to the precise nature of that form of fiction we call autobiography — because it is now universally accepted that autobiography *is* a fictional form, and an intriguing one — studies of autobiographical form, intention, or vision in *Lives of Girls and Women* have begun to return full circle upon this issue, and this is true of the direction of other recent criticism of *Lives*, as we shall see. Whereas early reviewers were often more anxious to either assert or deny the autobiographical charge, depending on the reviewer's assessment of how "honest" the book was, recent critics working in this area are more concerned with *how* autobiographical form, material, and impulse might be seen to be working in *Lives of Girls and Women*. Robert Thacker's article, " 'So Shocking a Verdict in Real Life': Autobiography in Alice Munro's Stories" is representative, and in a related direction, throughout *Alice Munro* E.D. Blodgett tries to show the ways in which we might understand Munro's representation of the "core" of her own life through her fiction.

PHOTOGRAPHY, FICTIONAL SURFACES, AND FORMS OF REALISM

Many readers have noted that Munro uses photographs and photographers in several ways in her fiction; the most striking example in *Lives of Girls and Women*, of course, is the closing section, "Epilogue: The Photographer." Munro has often remarked on her love of the work of certain photographers, and of certain Canadian painters whose work suggests an almost hyperreal attention to the way things actually appear to us in the world. Among them is Ken Danby, the painter whose portrait "The Sunbather" illustrates the cover of *Who Do You Think You Are* (1978) — a cover that for many readers seems to capture in its surface and texture, at once seemingly "photographic" but also more widely representational, an essential quality in Munro's art. Struthers's "Alice Munro and the American South," mentioned above, discusses Munro's "visual or photographic imagination" (198) and cites the influence on Munro of a celebrated book, *Let Us Now Praise Famous Men* (1960), a collaboration between writer James Agee and photographer Walker Evans. Munro's close attention to the surfaces of ordinary life has led critics to carefully study both the kinds of heightened realism that Munro's art conveys, and, more specifically, the ways in which her uses of photography or of images and descriptions of photographic art function in her writing. This direction in Munro criticism is only part of a larger investigation in contemporary criticism of the ways in which writing renders reality. Lorraine M. York has selected Munro and three other major figures for her 1988 study, *"The Other Side of Dailiness": Photography in the Works of Alice Munro, Timothy Findley, Michael Ondaatje, and Margaret Laurence*, and Deborah Bowen pursues the issue in her recent comparative essay, "In Camera: The Developed Photographs of Margaret Laurence and Alice Munro."

FEMINISM

The reviews of *Lives of Girls and Women* that praised the book for its frank depiction of women's lives can now be seen as precursors to the more searching studies that feminist critics are currently making of this text. The theoretical frameworks that feminist studies are bringing to bear on Munro's as well as many other writers' work have been outlined above; the growing number of feminist studies of *Lives of Girls and Women* include Bronwen Wallace's "Women's Lives: Alice Munro," which considers the roles of women in other Munro stories as well; Juliann E. Fleenor's persuasive discussion, "Rape Fantasies and Initiation Rite: Female Imagination in *Lives of Girls and Women*"; and Lorna Irvine's admirable article, "Changing Is the Word I Want," in which she shows how Munro presents women's stories, their perceptions and experience of change and of their own bodies. Arguing against theories of the "authority" of texts and of their "fathering," Irvine proposes an alternate story of genesis:

> What I am arguing in terms of Munro's fiction is a different theory of narrative sequence. As is particularly clear in the content of such stories as "The Ottawa Valley" and the whole of *Lives of Girls and Women*, Munro dramatically illustrates, through each writer-narrator, the ways in which texts may be imagined as being mothered and the different emphases that result from imagining writing in such a way. By extension, I suggest that it may be worthwhile to look at all of Munro's work as structural as well as contextual revelations of women's bodies, ego boundaries, and social status. When we do so, we discover the importance of change in this fiction, whether it be represented by specific physical or social transformations, by the fluidity of the narrative boundaries, or by the aesthetic movement between secrecy and revelation. (110)

Other recent studies include Barbara Godard's discussion, " 'Heirs of the Living Body': Alice Munro and the Question of a Female Aesthetic" and Smaro Kamboureli's "The Body as Audience and Performance in the Writing of Alice Munro."

TEXTS AND TEXTUALITY

We began this survey by looking at the ways in which reviewers read *Lives of Girls and Women* as engaging autobiography and anecdote, as frank realism, as regional fiction, and as an honest account of girls' and women's experience. It is only appropriate to close by noting how recent criticism has begun to return us to the text itself, to the act and art of reading, and to a consideration of the ways in which Del Jordan, too, reads her life through her encounters with a series of texts. This approach to *Lives of Girls and Women* reflects a particular application of a general theory: that texts do not only simply stand still in order to report on reality to their readers — which would also seem to imply that texts always stand apart, at some distance from the realities they represent — but that our reading also embeds us in a more active encounter and exchange with the text, a process analogous to Del Jordan's reading of the various texts she encounters. As I write, the most recent book on Munro's work, E.D. Blodgett's *Alice Munro*, takes up this issue in a thoroughgoing manner, showing how we might trace Del's development by considering the texts *she* reads in the course of her evolution from protagonist into narrator: the lurid headlines of Uncle Benny's newspapers; her Uncle Craig's unfinished history of Wawanash County; the various theological texts that inform "Age of Faith"; the encyclopedias her mother sells; the novels Del reads in the town library; sex manuals, love letters, and operettas, for example. Del's transformations, in other words, are transformations in reading, which bring us back to a renewed appreciation of the art of the text — of its significance, its existence, and its performance as a text — in short, of its "textuality."

This kind of reading begins to bring the account of the critical reception of *Lives of Girls and Women* to a full circle. We return, although differently disposed, to the place we started: to a fascination with the book's verisimilitude, its wealth and precision of detail, its structure, and above all, to the force and form of Del Jordan's recreated, recollected transformations and to the ways in which we might read them. With the measure of incompleteness that necessarily attends every critical venture, we can now return to the work of art that we began with. That is as it should be.

Reading of the Text

FORM: THE NOVEL AND ITS STORIES

> ... I think I am essentially a short story writer. That is why any novel that I write will be said, in some quarters, to be short stories. (Metcalf 61)

When J.R. (Tim) Struthers asked Munro in a 1983 interview about the order in which she wrote sections of the book, she replied:

> OK. I remember that quite clearly. "Princess Ida" was the first. It was going to be a short story. Then I saw it was going to work into a novel, and then I went on and on writing what I thought was a novel. Then I saw that wasn't working. So I went back and picked out of that novel "Princess Ida" in its original form — I had changed it to make it into the novel — and I picked out "Age of Faith," "Changes and Ceremonies," and "Lives of Girls and Women." Then, having written all those separate sections, I wrote "Baptizing." Then I went back and wrote the first two sections, the one about Uncle Benny, "The Flats Road"... and "Heirs of the Living Body." And then I wrote the "Epilogue: The Photographer," which gave me *all* kinds of trouble. (24–25)

In Munro's explanation we can see some of the reasons for the book's related claims as a novel and as a book of stories. These are not contradictory claims: a chapter in a novel is not the opposite of a story in a book of stories.

There are several elements of *Lives of Girls and Women* that pull towards the centralizing form of a novel: a single narrative voice (although, as we will see, this might be a deceptive way to describe Del's narration); a single central character (although at times she is defined more fully by her reactions to another character, or to an event she observes rather than experiences); a relatively stable cast of surrounding characters, including Del's family (although Del's father and Owen, like Uncle Benny, recede to the Flats Road house for a good part of the time in which Del's experiences are centered in Jubilee, and each section of the book tends to focus on Del's experience with a different set of characters); a roughly chronological line of development, tracing Del's growth from childhood through adolescence; and a common setting in Jubilee and the surrounding countryside.

But many of the elements of *Lives of Girls and Women* pull in a different direction — towards the form of a book of stories (as distinct from a collection of stories). First, we might consider Munro's description of the way she wrote the book: as suggested in the book's title, which looks towards the lives of both girls *and* women, the connections and distances between mother and daughter radiate out from the centre of this narrative towards its beginning and end ("The Flats Road" and the last two sections) as Del explores her evolving relationship with her mother, the "Princess Ida" that Munro began with. As her material grew under her pen, we can see how the shape of this relationship became so prominent in the book it informs. From the nucleus and the transformations of "Princess Ida," Munro tells us, came the section preceding it and the two following it; then came "Baptizing," followed by the book's two opening sections; and finally, the closing "Epilogue."

The continuous narrative line that we follow through the novel is also reshaped by the alternating cadences of Del's voice. Not only does Del's voice convey the distances as well as the closeness between past and present, between a younger Del and an older Del recollecting her experience; it also conveys another, still older Del's insight into that *whole* process of growth and change, and this is the voice of Del the writer, who speaks of and through all of the younger and the older versions of Del presented to us. In fact, we are invited to read Del the writer — and not Munro — as the creator of this book, as distinct from Munro, the author, who creates Del the writer, who speaks to us through her earlier and later reincarnations.

We hear this synchronicity of voice, which cuts across the chronology of events in this book, more fluently than we apprehend the events Del narrates; and the events that Del narrates tend to organize themselves into what could often stand as self-contained stories. From section to section, from chapter to chapter, Del often reminds her readers of who characters are, how settings signify, or what time frame we are reading in. But Del's voice always invites us to migrate easily with her across the borders between past, present, and future, so that our sense of what happens to her becomes more episodic than strictly linear. In other words, the causal relations between events that usually form a plot line are strongly affected by the forces and forms of Del's voice. Her voice shapes the parts of the book into reports, stories, and insights into the experiences Del recalls in order to give herself shape, to define her life in ways that seem meaningful to her — to turn her life into a story so that she might learn its form. We follow Del's impulses to shape her experiences through the seemingly erratic rhythms of her narration — its leisurely pauses to linger over the details of a description, its abrupt shifts and turns to different scenes and episodes. Our process of reading this kind of narration immerses us in the kind of development Del imagines and creates: the shaping of an identity seeking to order incoherent experience into the forms of stories.[7]

Del's impulse to turn reality into fiction leads me to the importance of the many different kinds of stories in this book, and here we can begin to see one of the ways in which *Lives of Girls and Women*, like much contemporary writing, begins to look in towards its own nature, its own workings and significance as a fiction, just as much as it looks out towards the stages of Del's experiences growing up in Jubilee. Del's strong need to turn events in her life into episodes in a fiction — to transform her experiences into stories that might reveal the significance of both — suggests some of the connections between living a life and narrating a story, between hearing and recounting different versions of stories, and between understanding autobiography as truths about a life and autobiography as a life story. We should be aware from the beginning that Del is not only telling us the story of her life — a story that changes its meanings for Del as she tells it to us — but that she is also fascinated with the various kinds and forms of stories that other characters tell about their own past and about each other. Consider Del's stories about Uncle Benny, and the stories that will be told by the community about Madeleine after her departure in "The Flats Road"; Auntie Grace and Aunt Elspeth's stories about their youth, and Uncle Craig's history of

Wawanash County in "Heirs of the Living Body"; Del's mother's and her Uncle Bill's different stories about their childhood in "Princess Ida"; the versions of belief embraced or abandoned in "Age of Faith"; Mr. Chamberlain's stories of wartime Italy in the title story, and Del's private stories about her imagined romance with him; or the many luridly docudramatic, melodramatic, and pornographic stories told in the various texts that Del describes as she reads them. This emphasis on the origins, the narration, and the significance of stories, for Del and for other characters, invites us to reflect with Del on the nature of fiction as it reports, informs, and recreates reality, working its transformations so inconspicuously and yet consistently that we believe Del's stories as if they were "true" stories — true, that is, to their nature as fictions, and not only to the facts of Del's (or of Munro's) experience. At this level, *Lives of Girls and Women* is not simply composed of Del's stories about her life; it is also Del's story about the composition, and the lives, of stories.

I don't propose to resolve the debate over the form of *Lives of Girls and Women* here, but rather to open up the question so that the book can be read plurally, through its several ways of conveying its stories, chapters, or episodes, with their several ways of meaning. Munro herself has called *Lives of Girls and Women* both an "episodic novel" and a book in which "the sections could almost stand as short stories,"[8] and the book's early reviewers, as John Metcalf recalls, identified it as " 'Memoir, autobiography, novel, collection of short stories' " (60). In its generous possibilities as a novel *and* a book of short stories, *Lives of Girls and Women* widens the resonances of both forms.

"THE FLATS ROAD": UNCLE BENNY AND STORIES OF FAMILY

"The Flats Road" reads as a prelude to the other sections that make up *Lives of Girls and Women*. Del's recollections of Uncle Benny and his failed attempt at marriage begin to move her out of childhood and an unquestioned, unquestioning security in her family toward her book-long, lifelong process of correcting, interpreting, and narrating her own version and vision of reality. To make her explorations of Uncle Benny's world intelligible, we see Del drawing the most naïve, and soonest abandoned of her distinctions: those between the eccentric and the mundane, the idiosyncratic and the average, between the Flats Road community and that of Jubilee, between the family her eccentric "Uncle" Benny gains and loses, and her own family, in which she can securely anchor herself for the last time. Once these distinctions are drawn and then dissolved — and once Del begins to grow beyond her vision of the stark simplicities of the Flats Road world and to recollect the more complex realities of town life in Jubilee — Uncle Benny's cosmos will recede in scope and passion to become a marginal, seasonal vestige of Del's experience, but a recognizable, parallel world nonetheless: a world she describes as lying "alongside" her own, not separate, not opposite, but related (22).

In the opening of "The Flats Road" we can see Del looking back and correcting her memories at the elementary but crucial level of names. Del (who remains unnamed herself until the next section of the book) recalls catching frogs on the riverbank for Uncle Benny, and then immediately points out that Benny is not really family; the designation "Uncle" is a sign of familiarity, not of formal family relation: "He was not our Uncle, or anybody's" (1). A similar process quickly recurs as Del recalls Uncle Benny's reprimand:

> "You kids want to splash in the mud and scare off the fish you go and do it someplace else, get off my riverbank."
> It was not his. Right here, where he usually fished, it was ours. But we never thought of that. (1)

Uncle Benny also provides Del with the occasion for the first of her many excursions into the wider world conjured by words, even when she misapprehends them. Early in the story she remembers him describing the Grenoch Swamp, with its "quicksand hole . . . that would take down a two-ton truck like a bite of breakfast" (1), and then recalls herself constructing a visual image from the sound of the word: "(In my mind I saw it shining, with a dry-liquid roll — I had it mixed up with quicksilver)" (2).[9]

Uncle Benny is familiar to Del because he works for her father raising silver foxes and eats with her family; but he also stands at the centre of a seemingly self-contained world that Del is drawn to and wonders at, and he is a collector of miscellaneous clutter who provides her with endless pleasure as she tries to list the improbable contents of his house. The decrepit but endlessly fascinating jumble that Uncle Benny lives within marks him as both eccentric and domestic, comically arcane in his habits and failed business ventures, but also a compulsive and hopeful preserver of the broken down and the ordinary, of other people's discards as well as his own. As Del remarks, the clutter in the house stands as a reminder of domesticity: "So part of the accumulation was that of fifty years or so of family life" (4).

But the most enticing of Uncle Benny's possessions for Del is the lurid newspaper he subscribes to, and this is another way in which "The Flats Road" provides us with an important entrance into Del's larger story: these newspapers, with their melodramatic, fragmented headlines, announcing grotesque, improbable, or simply fantastical "news" from the world beyond Jubilee, function on several levels as they engross Del's imagination. First, Del makes it clear that the world reported on in these newspapers — the "only source of information about the outside world" for Uncle Benny (4) — is not the world her parents read about in their newspapers, the Jubilee *Herald-Advance* or the city newspaper they receive. Information about that world consists either of the very sketchy history of the war, which "had started by that time," or of events of political or purely local interest — "elections, or heat waves, or accidents" (4). Throughout *Lives of Girls and Women*, Del will recall news of the world beyond Jubilee, particularly of the war, as a thin emanation; her consciousness forms itself through an intense curiosity about the local, ordinary surfaces of the immediate world around her, *and* through her intense curiosity about the worlds revealed to her in texts — usually, as is the case in this section, worlds far removed from her everyday experience.[10]

Second, Del's attraction to these headlines alerts us both to her fascination with reading, and to the ways in which she constructs and discards alternate realities through her reading. For Del, with her essentially verbal imagination, reading becomes a crucial way of organizing reality, a means by which she can begin to establish either connections or distances between her immediate experience and the events reported in texts; further, reading provides her with one way of assessing what is "true" in experience. Uncle Benny, in several ways a less able reader than Del, is shown to inhabit his eccentric world largely as a result of this inability; maps of cities prove to be just as indecipherable to him as do the manners and motivations of his wife.

In "The Flats Road" it is easy for us to be more discriminating readers than Del; it was less easy for her at this point in her life, she recalls, to accommodate both what the headlines report to her and what her everyday experience conveys. For Del, the headlines announce an alluring disruption of the ordinary. She is acutely aware, too, not only of their qualities as texts, but also of their texture, their material nature, and this is a quality that the text of *Lives of Girls and Women* itself brings to readers' attention here and throughout the book, with its frequent quotations from the texts that Del remembers reading:

> His paper came once a week and was printed badly on rough paper with headlines three inches high. . . .
> FATHER FEEDS TWIN DAUGHTERS TO HOGS
> WOMAN GIVES BIRTH TO HUMAN MONKEY
> VIRGIN RAPED ON CROSS BY CRAZED MONKS
> SENDS HUSBAND'S TORSO BY MAIL (4)

This tabloid version of the news is only one of the several credulous but passionately held worldviews that compose Uncle Benny's conception of reality, and it is interesting that the same newspaper will also be the vehicle through which Uncle Benny learns of and sends for Madeleine, his wife to be. The realities proposed by the headlines inflame Del's curiosity, and yet she knows that these are "realities" only possible to conceive, only credible, while she is within the parallel world of Uncle Benny's house and its claims on her imagination:

> I read faster and faster, all I could hold, then reeled out into the sun, onto the path that led to our place, across the fields. I was bloated and giddy with revelations of evil, of its versatility and grand invention and horrific playfulness. But the nearer I got to our house the more this vision faded. Why was it that the plain back wall of home, the pale chipped brick, the cement platform outside the kitchen door, washtubs hanging on nails, the pump, the lilac bush with brown-spotted leaves, should make it seem doubtful that a woman would really send her husband's torso, wrapped in Christmas paper, by mail to his girl friend in South Carolina? (4–5)

The texts that Del reads at Uncle Benny's announce stories from a world that she cannot accommodate within the flat, pale, but safe enclosure that her parents' house provides her. The headlines' texts must be relegated to a world most vivid in the imagination, while the Flats Road world — a world in which Uncle Benny sits at the Jordan family dinner table, a familiar, almost childlike companion who sticks his chewing gum on the end of his fork while he eats — provides Del with ample material for the richly detailed descriptions of the surfaces of the real world she lives in. These two complementary impulses in Del's consciousness — to read texts in order to imagine worlds, and to describe the world she sees before her eyes in order to construct a coherent reality — converge in "The Flats Road" as in the other sections of *Lives of Girls and Women* through Del's fascination with the shapes of the stories that she reads, hears, and learns how to tell.

The importance of reading and writing in connection with stories related or experienced becomes clearer to us as Uncle Benny enlists Del's help in responding to the advertisement for a husband that he has read in the newspaper. When he asks Del for a sample of her writing, her written response, as several readers have noted, recalls Stephen Daedalus's widening spirals of identification when he writes his name in an often-quoted scene from *A Portrait of the Artist as a Young Man*;[11] in Joyce and in Munro, the process of naming would seem to correspond to a process of location, a naming of place, through which a sense of self is constructed verbally and materially from its situation in ever-widening spheres; here, Del is naming Uncle Benny, as if to suggest her own abiding curiosity about his identity:

> *Mr. Benjamin Thomas Poole, The Flats Road, Jubilee, Wawanash County, Ontario, Canada, North America, The Western Hemisphere, The World, The Solar System, The Universe.* (9)

The improbable story of Uncle Benny's short-lived marriage to Madeleine is anticipated by the gothic story that he tells the Jordans, before Madeleine's arrival, about Sandy Stevenson's haunted marriage on the Flats Road (8). Now we see through Del's eyes how Uncle Benny's own marriage will be transformed into a story, one that will be repeated until it becomes soothing and familiar, so that

Madeleine's unpredictable violence and her beating of her daughter become part of the Flats Road community's lore. "The Flats Road" closes with Del's suggestive remarks about recollections transformed into fiction: "Madeleine herself was like something he [Uncle Benny] might have made up. We remembered her like a story, and having nothing else to give we gave her our strange, belated, heartless applause" (23). Remembering characters and events like stories is an apt way to describe the process through which Del shapes her experiences; in this opening section, remembering Madeleine like a story allows her to shape the connections between her family and Uncle Benny's, and between her family and herself, into the beginnings of a story that accommodates apparently contradictory settings and realities as well as apparently contradictory senses of family.

Finally, all of Del's recollections and stories about Uncle Benny cumulate in her description of herself at the end of the story, where she is poised at the edge of her childhood, remembering the security she felt within her family and the Flats Road world. In the closing passages of "The Flats Road" Del the writer — the narrator who was that little girl and who has written *Lives of Girls and Women* — reflects on the kind of familiarity and "connection" (a recurring word in Munro's fiction) she feels within her family, and also, in turn, to her family's connection to Uncle Benny and to the Flats Road:

> My mother sat in her canvas chair and my father in a wooden one; they did not look at each other. But they were connected, and this connection was plain as a fence, it was between us and Uncle Benny, us and the Flats Road, it would stay between us and anything. (22)

In the emphatic, almost defiant rhythms of Del's assertions we might sense the unease that prompts her affirmation of connection, as if this were also Del's affirmation of the beginning of the end of her childhood, a last and fond look back at that time in her life when she could brave the darkness and fall asleep alone even if it seemed "miles above" her parents downstairs, where they played cards in the kitchen and emanated a sense of security in their very ordinariness — "prosaic as a hiccup, familiar as breath" (22). Her insight into Uncle Benny's world, her (textual) participation in Uncle Benny's venture into marriage, and in its transformation into a story, all turn

Del toward her own experience, toward the question of how she will name herself and shape her experiences in subsequent sections of the book.

"The Flats Road," written after "Princess Ida" and the middle sections of the book, also shows how Munro uses her settings to define the relationships between characters and to evoke her communities. The stark distinctions that Del draws in this story between the Flats Road and Jubilee, and between her parents' perspectives on these communities, begin to establish the frame of reference for the book's extended exploration of her evolving relationship with her mother. Here, the outlines of this relationship are sketched in, and their future development predicted, through Del's descriptions of her mother's attitude towards both town and countryside:

> My mother corrected me when I said we lived on the Flats Road; she said we lived *at the end* of the Flats Road, as if that made all the difference. Later on she was to find that she did not belong in Jubilee either . . . . (6)

Del distinguishes at this point between her mother and father largely in terms of their perspectives on the Flats Road world; her father, who has conserved his country background while Del's mother has abandoned hers, feels much more comfortable on the Flats Road, less so in Jubilee. As Del looks back on her parents' sense of place — at this point, described as reflections of their senses of themselves — she begins to sketch in the tensions between her mother and herself that will develop more fully in later episodes. Del recalls that when she and her mother walked into Jubilee from the Flats Road, her mother's hopeful and cheery greetings, received at a polite distance in Jubilee, did not register on the girl she then was, but also suggests that this would change: "As yet I followed her without embarrassment, enjoying the commotion" (7). And in an equally telling observation of her mother at the dinner table, catching her in a rare unguarded moment as she responds to her husband's wry and gentle prodding of Uncle Benny, Del describes her both then, in the Flats Road world of Del's youth, and as the woman she would become:

> . . . she had these unpredictable moments of indulgence, lost later on, when the very outlines of her body seemed to soften and her

indifferent movements, lifting of the plates, had an easy supremacy. She was a fuller, fairer woman than she later became. (9)

In these two passages we can see clear illustrations of the fluidity with which Del's narration moves between the narrative present she is remembering — the Flats Road world she lived in as a girl, catching frogs for Uncle Benny, reading newspaper headlines on his porch, writing his letter of proposal for him — and the seeds of the narrative future contained within these recollections, the suggestions of what her mother would become, of what her responses to her mother would become. Both narrative lines run pastwards from the perspective of Del the writer, and in "The Flats Road" as much as in the other parts of *Lives of Girls and Women*, both perspectives seem to be natural reflections of Del's character. Later sections will show us how much artifice it takes to make Del's perspective seem natural and how much art to make her experiences seem real.

"HEIRS OF THE LIVING BODY": THE DEATH OF A HISTORY

For the most part, the first three chapters of *Lives of Girls and Women* — "The Flats Road," "Heirs of the Living Body," and "Princess Ida" — show us Del recalling her responses to events in which other characters, or forces beyond Del's control, play the major part. In these chapters, Del is just as much a witness to as an actor in the events she recalls. And Del's recollections of the events that might seem to form the backbone of a plot — Uncle Benny's marriage, Uncle Craig's death, Uncle Bill's visit to Jubilee — are never straightforward, never chronological. We arrive at the major episodes of each story via a circuitous route, through a labyrinth of detail, of recollected incidents and stories, through Del's insights into character, her descriptions of setting, and the sweep of her perspective as it ranges over her past. What we learn about Del, and what Del learns about herself in these early sections, accumulates mainly through the insights Del gains into others' realities. Her story has not yet turned inwards toward her own resolutions about the ways in which she will shape her own life or understand her own experience. In "Heirs of the Living Body," the indirections of Del's narration culminate in the insight that Del gains and will later act on by writing *Lives of Girls and Women*: she realizes that Uncle Craig's unfinished history of Wawanash County, a literal and documentary account of the past written as an objective record, cannot bring the past alive in the ways that fiction can.

This might seem an incidental or even a trivial insight for Del at this point in her narration. "Heirs of the Living Body" might seem to be more centrally focussed on Del's encounters with mortality, and certainly these are important elements. As well, there does seem to be an implied progression from the episode in which Mary Agnes Oliphant and Del come upon the dead cow (and Mary Agnes surprises Del by laying her hand over the cow's eye) to Uncle Craig's funeral and Del's resistance to seeing his body (and Mary Agnes's role in this scene). And this chapter does begin to round this book towards its shape as a novel by providing us with the first full portraits of Del's family, particularly of her mother and of Aunt Elspeth and Auntie Grace.

On first reading, we might also be drawn to the significance of Del's account of her mother's worldview, particularly her view of mortality, since the chapter takes its title from the magazine article that Del's mother has been reading, and Del transcribes in full her mother's lecture concerning limited human perceptions of death. But in Del's evocations of Uncle Craig and his work, we are also invited to discern another of this book's explorations of the meanings and forms of stories and, in this case, of histories. The portraits of Del's aunts, the episodes with Mary Agnes, Del's mother's sermons, and Uncle Craig's death itself all contribute to Del's closing insight into what Uncle Craig was compiling as a life work — and what kind of mistake this kind of writing might be for *her* imagination.

In "Heirs of the Living Body" we can also see how the sweep of time afforded by Del's fluid shifts in perspective transcends straight chronology. Uncle Craig dies when Del is a young girl, shortly after her return to Jubilee from a visit to Jenkins' Bend, and much of the story is set in that time of Del's life. But this temporal setting distends in several ways — towards several levels and layers of the past, through the stories the aunts tell of their own earlier experiences, and through Uncle Craig's construction of a family tree and his history of Wawanash County; and towards several layers of Del's own future, through the many ways in which she suggests the evolution of her own insights into the experiences she is recollecting, culminating with her memory of herself in high school, when Uncle Craig's manuscript is destroyed by the flooding of her basement. We are told very early in the story that Uncle Craig is "displeased" with Del because of her "inaccurate notions of time and history" (24–25), an attitude that we might read somewhat ironically, given Uncle Craig's view of the past as a lockstep march of events in succession, and given Del's own practices as a narrator and a writer. In fact, one of the crucial stages in Del's initiation, as for many of Munro's characters, will be her education in the meanings of time, an education begun most clearly in this story through her setting aside Uncle Craig's notions of history.[12]

The language of her narration also shows how an older Del merges with and emerges from younger versions of herself as she remembers her past. At the funeral, Del recalls the men outside the house "walking on the hay stubble, all in dark suits like tall crows, talking" (43); the men in the hall, she remembers, were "like tree trunks to work your way through" (43). The similes evoke the vocabulary, perspective, and imagination of a young girl. But at many other points in the narration, Del's language will evoke an older narrator — one who can recall eating a "surreptitious breakfast" (38), or who can generalize about behaviour as Del does throughout the book; here, she offers this insight into her mother's insistence that she go to the funeral:

> Her briskness and zeal seemed false and vulgar. I did not trust her. Always when people tell you you will have to face this sometime, when they hurry you matter-of-factly towards whatever pain or obscenity or unwelcome revelation is laid out for you, there is this edge of betrayal, this cold, masked, imperfectly hidden jubilation in their voices, something greedy for your hurt. Yes, in parents too; in parents particularly. (39–40)

This is the insight of an older narrator into the deceptions that adults — parents in particular — practice on children. It is not the perception of a child who might feel a vague sense of unease, hurt, or betrayal as a result of an adult's behaviour.

Through Del's depictions of Uncle Craig, Aunt Elspeth, and Auntie Grace, Munro begins to develop a vital element in the texture of *Lives of Girls and Women*: its recurrent examination of women's views of men and their work. Interestingly, we see this exploration developed in two ways — through Uncle Craig's sisters' attitudes, and through Del's reading. The sisters' attitudes to their brother's work are ambivalent but assured:

> They respected men's work beyond anything; they also laughed at it. This was strange; they could believe absolutely in its importance and at the same time convey their judgement that it was, from one point of view, frivolous, nonessential. And they would never, never meddle with it; between men's work and women's work was the clearest line drawn, and any stepping over this line, any suggestion of stepping over it, they would meet with such light, amazed, regretfully superior, laughter. (27)

In the closing of Del's description of her aunts' attitude, we can see how Munro will deploy a series of adjectives, each one adding a divergent qualification, to convey the contradictions inherent in this kind of perception — often, a perception of someone else's that Del recalls, but one that Del will also correct or transform as she describes it and, partly through this very process of describing it, gain insight into it as well. Del's more fully revised perception of her aunts' attitude comes to her years later, through her reading a passage in *War and Peace* (in another example of Del reading her past through other texts, this time, through a novel): "When I read, years afterwards, about Natasha in *War and Peace*, and how she *ascribed immense importance, although she had no understanding of them, to her husband's abstract, intellectual pursuits*, I had to think of Aunt Elspeth and Auntie Grace" (27).

Through Del's recollections of her aunts, we can begin to appreciate the constraints that Del senses in their distrust of ambition — a censure that will embrace Del's mother, too, and that will recur in several guises throughout the novel as Del tries to define and affirm her own vision. But the aunts' reverence for Uncle Craig's history, like their assessment of ambition, must finally seem misplaced to us because of its implication that they are misreading Del's character and the directions she will take. Unlike Uncle Craig or her cousin Ruth McQueen, both of whom seem to echo Melville's Bartleby — they "preferred not" to pursue opportunities, Del is instructed by her aunts (32) — Del determines to pursue a vocation, even though she does not realize until much later that her calling will return her precisely to the territory that Uncle Craig has inhabited in his way for his whole life.

Aside from their importance as storytellers, Aunt Elspeth and Auntie Grace also serve to reveal the complex of manners, perceptions, and attitudes that comprise the subtle but powerful social codes of Jubilee and the surrounding countryside — codes that Del's mother is either blissfully unaware of or aggressively challenges. Del's perception of her mother's blundering up against Del's aunts' norms (and, later, Jubilee norms as well) begins to establish the foundations for her mother's idiosyncrasies — turns of mind that Del both admires and rebels from. The development of her mother's character, its outlines already traced in "The Flats Road," now is set against the characters of Del's aunts, who provide Del with a different set of conventions, and a different repository of stories through which to understand her reality. Her mother lectures, proselytizes, and pronounces, taking a direct but often blinkered route to what she perceives as the truth about convention or conduct; the aunts quietly circle, nudging Del through whispers, irony, and indirection, their implied censure of her mother's indiscretions educating Del in small but sharp cuts. The social world that Del is growing into is still at this point in the book comprised mainly of concentric rings of family, of uncles and aunts and cousins, as it will be in the next chapter; in their intuitive adherence to convention, their quiet assurance, their prodigious but predictable energy, and their comfort in their setting and tradition, Aunt Elspeth and Auntie Grace seem to serve as instructive counterpoints to Del's mother. But their influence on Del wanes after Uncle Craig's death and, more importantly, after she arrives at her assessment of his perception of the past.

If we are looking for a way of defining the plot of "Heirs of the Living Body," we might first be tempted to fasten on its exploration of Del's encounters with mortality. This way of characterizing this section would lead us to similar conceptions of later chapters, so that we could read *Lives of Girls and Women* as a series of depictions of the progressive, sequential stages in Del's growth. In Del's encounter with the dead cow, we can see how the episode reveals the various ways, all of them in some measure unsuccessful, in which Del tries to perceive or imagine the reality of death, but finds that it always defies her grasp. Her first, imaginative conception of the cow transforms its hide into a meaningful pattern — a map, over which Del will have control, since she has invested it with meaning:

> I could see that the cow's hide was a map. The brown could be the ocean, the white the floating continents. With my stick I traced their strange shapes, their curving coasts, trying to keep the point of the stick exactly between the white and the brown. (37)

But this first effort fails when she gets to the eye, because it will not yield its central but mysterious implication that Del is actually contemplating a form of life that once had an expression, an eye that once saw, and that now she can only describe. In fact, description itself becomes a kind of defense for Del, as if by imagining the eye in other terms, she might be able to protect herself from its actual import:

> The eye was wide open, dark, a smooth sightless bulge, with a sheen like silk and a reddish gleam in it, a reflection of light. An orange stuffed in a black silk stocking. Flies nestled in one corner, bunched together beautifully in an iridescent brooch. (37)

Both of these first efforts to distance herself from the death of the cow, from its mysterious and yet palpable, visible signs of mortality, now yield to another angle of attack: Del would like to poke the eye, to see what it concealed beneath its shiny surface. But she cannot bring herself to come into such intimate contact with such unknowable realities — particularly since they are realities announced by and through the body — and therefore has recourse to her most constant, most natural medium: language itself. There are numerous examples in this story of Del's recurrent tendency to conjure and to create reality by proceeding in her imagination from words to the worlds they evoke: consider, for example, her conception of the words "birth canal" (33–34), of the meanings of Orange Hall or Blue River (39), or her contemplation of the word "*died*," of Uncle Craig's "Heart *attack*" (39), or of her mother's use of "barbaric" (47). Looking at the dead cow, Del seizes on the words themselves, ignoring Mary Agnes' warning: " 'Day-ud cow,' I said, expanding the word lusciously. 'Day-ud cow, day-ud cow' " (37).[13]

But the mystery of this animal's death, its silent (and wordless) and menacing significance, refuses to yield to Del's various stratagems. She would like to assault the cow's body in its immobility, attack its very existence: but in Del's defiance, in the very strength of her aggression we can sense her baffled rage:

> Being dead, it invited desecration. I wanted to poke it, trample it, pee on it, anything to punish it, to show what contempt I had for its being dead. Beat it, break it up, spit on it, tear it, throw it away! But still it had power, lying with a gleaming strange map on its back, its straining neck, the smooth eye. (38)

None of the fictions and none of the words that Del has interposed like screens between her and the cow succeed in making its death comprehensible, admissible, and she is left, as she so often is in her narration, with an irreducible mystery that will not yield to explanation, that must be shaped into a story. The mystery revealed to Del in "The Flats Road" is Uncle Benny's bizarre but enchanted world, in which "nothing was deserved, anything might happen" (22); the mere idiosyncrasy of Uncle Benny's reality, however — which Del can in some measure assimilate as a world lying "alongside" her own — does not present her with the more formidable and universal riddle posed by the dead cow. It is at the same time irrevocably dead and unfathomably singular; it cannot be duplicated or repeated, and it cannot be defended against. In death, paradoxically, it announces the mystery of individual being:

> I had never once looked at a cow alive and thought what I thought now: why should there be a cow? Why should the white spots be shaped just the way they were, and never again, not on any cow or creature, shaped in exactly the same way? . . . I paid attention to its shape . . . as if the shape itself were a revelation beyond words, and I would be able to make sense of it, if I tried hard enough, and had time. (38)

What Del is discovering, in a rhythm that will recur throughout *Lives of Girls and Women*, is the limits of the knowable world. Her driving curiosity is always fueled by a burning desire to *know*, because, as she says when she pursues her mother around the house after being told of Uncle Craig's death, "There is no protection, unless it is in knowing" (39). But what her experience all too often teaches her, as she is confronted with inexplicable mystery, is that she *cannot* know. And hard on the heels of this discovery she is confronted with Mary Agnes's own mysterious and unpredictable action as she places her hand over the dead cow's eye (38).

Del is shown another way of knowing, of seeming to explain away what is irreducibly mysterious, by her mother. But her mother's lecture only serves to teach Del that this kind of explanation, this relentless, cheerful rationalization, only produces its own bafflement: it will not shield Del from Uncle Craig's body and its inexplicable presence. And the episode at the funeral shows us that Del both needs and flees a separate apprehension of mortality, and that her route to knowledge will be more intuitive and more visceral than her mother's disembodied maxims allow for.

Trying to define the plot of a Munro story or chapter in the way outlined above, however, often turns into a wild goose chase, because in many Munro stories a plot formed by a causally linked chain of events is replaced by a series of more casually, more tenuously linked episodes that, through their indirect relationships with each other, culminate in an insight or revelation for Del. In fact, their intentional dispersals of well-formed plots are among the structural and cultural signs that identify Munro's stories as contemporary fiction. As is true of all the chapters in *Lives of Girls and Women*, the stories that Del hears in "Heirs of the Living Body" from other characters, as well as about other characters, form one series of episodes that will culminate in her insight into Uncle Craig's history and its deficiencies. And acknowledging the workings of this "plot," rather than concentrating only on the sequence formed by Del's two encounters with mortality, might enrich our reading of this chapter and of the book. We hear Aunt Elspeth's and Auntie Grace's stories of their youth (28–29); Uncle Craig's recollections of the past (24–25); Aunt Moira's stories of Porterfield (34–35), as well as Del's mother's stories about Mary Agnes's birth (33–34), and about Mary Agnes's abuse at the hands of the five boys (36); Del's mother's lecture on mortality and on organ transplants (40–41); and, of course, all of Del's recollections as they form the shape of the larger story she is narrating. This series culminates in Aunt Elspeth and Auntie Grace handing over Uncle Craig's unfinished history to Del.

It is difficult to read Del's aunts' instructions and comments in this scene without quickly becoming aware of how Del is hearing them; the irony of the situation, the distance that we feel we have come from Del's earlier, less ambivalent admiration for her aunts, marks the distance Del herself has come in this chapter. The excerpt that Del reads from the history (51) teaches her that this conception of the past yields a lifeless, inert document, a language and vision that signal another, no less powerfully apprehended kind of death for a reader like Del. And so it is fitting that, after first keeping the box with the manuscript under her bed, and putting her own writing in the box for safekeeping, she should fear that one kind of writing might contaminate the other:

> I didn't want Uncle Craig's manuscript put back with the things I had written. It seemed so dead to me, so heavy and dull and useless, that I thought it might deaden my things too and bring me bad luck. (52)

Once Del has arrived at this perception, we can read her response to the destruction of Uncle Craig's manuscript as a testament both to her regret at not fulfilling her aunts' wishes — at not being the kind of person, the kind of writer they would have wished — and as the more dominant and necessary assertion of her own purpose: "I thought of them watching the manuscript leave their house in its padlocked box and I felt remorse, that kind of tender remorse which has on its other side a brutal, unblemished satisfaction" (53).

"Heirs of the Living Body" shows us Del recalling several related encounters: with the mystery of mortality, and with the inadequacy of some kinds of knowing — her own, her mother's, Uncle Craig's, among others. She has yet to discover that stories, too, may turn out to be unreliable, unverifiable, and ultimately mysterious in their translations of experience.

"PRINCESS IDA": A MOTHER'S STORIES RETOLD

In the two opening chapters of *Lives of Girls and Women*, Del reveals several different facets of her mother's character, but the focus of

A draft of the beginning of "Princess Ida."

Special Collections, University of Calgary Libraries.

"The Flats Road" and "Heirs of the Living Body" lies elsewhere. In "Princess Ida" — the section that, Munro tells us, was first a story, then began growing into a novel, and then reverted to its original form — Del turns more directly to her memories of her mother, exploring Addie Morrison's character more fully than in any other chapter in the book. Through its concentrated focus on Del's mother, this section serves as a major turning point for Del in her recollections of her life within her family. We might see, as well, how and why this chapter should have been the origin and then become the nucleus of the whole book. On one level, Del's mother represents a way of being and of seeing that Del embraces, identifies, and finally discards in her progress towards a more autonomous identity; this process reflects the tensions we might expect between a mother and daughter who will eventually find themselves so much at odds over what constitutes a girl's or a woman's identity, vision, and story. But on another level, Del's mother has a more important, if more indirect function in this chapter and in the whole book. In "Princess Ida," Del learns more about the ways in which stories conjure and reshape the past. More importantly, she learns that stories may have an entirely different value as revelations of character and vision. In this chapter, Del learns about her mother by learning about how her mother tells stories — stories that, as Del puts it in another passage often quoted in discussions of Munro's fiction, "could go ... round and round and down to death; I expected it" (66).

Composed as it is of Del's mother's pen name, the title of this chapter immediately raises the question of Addie's identity and reminds us that she sees herself in frames of reference that must seem suspiciously exotic in Jubilee, as well as to her own daughter. And the primacy of texts in this story (and of Del's mother's activities as seen from a Jubilee perspective) is neatly, comically, and economically established in the story's opening sentences: "Now my mother was selling encyclopedias. Aunt Elspeth and Auntie Grace called it 'going on the road!'" (54) "Now" can be read both as a chronological signal — a signal of time passing, of Del now being older than the girl who bites Mary Agnes's arm in "Heirs of the Living Body" — and as an expression of Del's retrospective bemusement at her mother's idiosyncrasy, a pitch of voice and turn of phrase that anticipate her aunts' snide remark.

Del's memories of her mother selling encyclopedias, and of her own participation in this venture, are fitting episodes with which to open this story. First, we are made aware of her mother's perspective on the kind of knowledge assembled and preserved in an encyclopedia, and of how and why her mother values this information. It is difficult, in fact, not to see Addie Morrison's love for encyclopedias as related to her love for crossword puzzles, and to recall that the chapter ends with Del recounting her sudden insight into her mother's feelings while her mother works on a crossword puzzle. For Addie, knowledge is a social weapon as well as a sign of good breeding, to be deployed in the name either of progressive values and attitudes, or as a valuable possession, an endowment to be drawn upon in parlour games. At the opening of this story, Del treasures the encyclopedia, seeing it as a text imbued with all of the nostalgic, romantic gloom of history rendered as a kind of authoritative melodrama. Again, we are reminded of how texts present themselves to Del as tangible and substantial, as if the realities that they evoked were intimately connected to their material reality. It is worth quoting an extended passage from early in the story to illustrate just how fully and to what effects Del's powers of description are often trained on the appearance of the texts she reads:

> I loved the volumes of the encyclopedia, their weight (of mystery, of beautiful information), as they fell open in my lap; I loved their sedate dark-green binding, the spidery, reticent-looking gold letters on their spines. They might open to show me a steel engraving of a battle, taking place on the moors, say, with a castle in the background, or in the harbor of Constantinople. All bloodshed, drowning, hacking off of heads, agony of horses, was depicted with a kind of operatic flourish, a superb unreality. And I had the impression that in historical times the weather was always theatrical, ominous; landscape frowned, sea glimmered in various dull or metallic shades of gray. (55–56)

Del's imagination fastens first on the material nature and appearance of the texts — their binding, their lettering — and then seizes on their content, which is depicted with an "operatic flourish, a superb unreality." Evoked in this phrase is one of the paradoxes that pervade Del's narration: that reality can so often be textually recreated in a melodramatic, "operatic" (or "theatrical") style that she at once recognizes as a kind of "unreality" *and* as "superb." She glories, in other words, in the form of the encyclopedia because it announces its artifice; it makes history "operatic," but it also makes it knowable. Because Del has a superb, if not an encyclopedic memory, she can quickly recall details and lists for her mother in potential clients' houses.

But in the first of the linked transformations Del undergoes in this chapter, she becomes acutely embarrassed by her own pose, her own appearance as she nonchalantly recites lists of American presidents for prospective buyers. She is responding to the social register that her mother, seemingly as a matter of principle, almost never acknowledges, putting Del's reactions down to " 'Shyness and self-consciousness' " (57). But Del's response is also an instinctive, intuitive act of concealment, not from her mother's clients, but from her mother herself. It is the first of a series of differentiating gestures that Del will make in the course of her narration, many of them revealed in a response to texts, stories, or the stories she reads in texts. She cannot bring herself to recite memorized facts from the encyclopedia because the encyclopedia (and what it entails) is really her mother's domain. It contains a world of knowledge that, in ways related to the knowledge imparted by Uncle Craig's history, is not going to be very useful for her own, as yet undiscerned project. And it is knowledge that is conveyed in a form far more indicative of her mother's codes of conduct and manner of being than of her own.

We must recognize, though, that Del's relationship with her mother is charged with ambivalences that Del herself acknowledges in retrospect from the very beginning of the book. Del does not simply record the evolution of her connections to her mother as they modulate into more keenly perceived distances; she also recalls how strongly she cleaved to her mother, how she depended upon her mother to bestow on Del a sense of place as well as a sense of the past, and Del recalls both of these impulses more clearly here than in any other part of the novel.

For Del and her younger brother Owen, the drive home to Jubilee from their excursions with their mother as she sells encyclopedias is always marked by their mother's welcomed authority to announce their homecoming. Del's description of the physical appearance of Jubilee (57–58) as they approach the town from the highway adopts something of the same perspective through which Del describes the dead cow's hide as a map in "Heirs of the Living Body." It is a perspective that is at once detached, wondering, and welcoming, and also a perspective authorized in large part by her mother. It is at one level a perspective that recalls Del's remark a page earlier about the children's attitude to the landscape: "We drove through country we did not know we loved" (57). And yet the detail with which Del evokes both the countryside and Jubilee stands as evidence of two related impulses: first, the strong identification with and love of place (a love that Del has not yet named at this point, a love she only discovers in retrospect as she recalls these drives home), and second, her writer's impulse, named and acknowledged in "Epilogue: The Photographer," to record "every last thing" (210) about Jubilee and her past, about the ways in which Jubilee and her own past are inextricably bound up in each other. At this point in the novel, these impulses coexist without great tension, as Del faithfully records the surfaces of what she sees. But at the same time, overseeing her recreations of her younger incarnations, she also acknowledges the depths or the mysteries beneath these closely catalogued surfaces. So the most comfortable perspective for Del to adopt in order to describe Jubilee is slightly distanced — a perspective from the highway, from where she can see the town's whole shape at dusk, as "more or less that of a bat, one wing lifted slightly, bearing the water tower, unlighted, indistinct, on its tip" (58).

Del's perspective on her mother's power establishes a connection between how Del describes setting at this point and what kind of control her mother exerts over her children. Del's descriptions are evocations rendered within her mother's dominion; and Del acknowledges her mother's power from a perspective that announces Del's insight into these relations between daughter and mother, relations that become apparent to Del through her recollections of this time of her life and through the kinds of descriptions that these recollections produce. What Del is discovering is how her recollection produces both an image of a setting and, just as importantly in a novel about the development of a writer's imagination, an intuition that leads to an articulated insight into her own state of mind — an insight related from the perspective of an older Del. The stages of this process are exemplified as Del describes, first her mother's responses to Jubilee, then her response to her mother and to Jubilee, and finally her insight into her mother's status:

> My mother would never let this sighting go by without saying something. "There's Jubilee," she might say simply, or, "Well, yonder lies the metropolis," or she might even quote, fuzzily, a poem about going in the same door as out she went. And by these words, whether weary, ironic, or truly grateful, Jubilee seemed to me to take its being. As if without her connivance, her acceptance, these streetlights and sidewalks, the fort in the wilderness, the open and secret pattern of the town — a shelter and a mystery — would not be there. Over all our expeditions, and homecomings, and the world at large, she exerted this mysterious, appalling authority, and nothing could be done about it, not yet. (58)

Del recalls, first, the various ways in which her mother announces their return to Jubilee, quoting her mother's different turns of phrase, which progress from simple statement of fact, to inflated, mock-poetic diction, to a half-remembered quotation from a poem — a strategy that "Princess Ida" might well adopt. Then Del, always keenly aware of verbal resonances, acknowledges that it is "by these words," by her mother's various tonal and verbal formulations, that Jubilee seemed to her then to "take its being"; her mother has the power to summon Jubilee into existence for Del by naming it in several ways. But Del also recognizes that this perception of her mother's power is, and was, a child's perception, and she registers this insight in the opening of the next sentence: it is only *"As if"* her mother really had this power to name Jubilee for her children. Del the writer now has fuller access to words, to names of her own devising to assemble as she looks back on Jubilee and the many layers of meaning that reside within it. Her own description of Jubilee, with its modulating, evolving qualifications defining and redefining Jubilee as a "fort in the wilderness," then a town with both an "open and secret pattern," and finally a town that is both a "shelter and a mystery," is a fine illustration of Del's characteristic way of presenting seemingly opposed definitions as if they were compatible. She is forming a vision, as Helen Hoy and several other Munro critics have suggested, that accommodates paradoxes, just as in the first chapter it eventually accommodates both Uncle Benny's and her own family's worlds.

The other large area over which Del's mother exerts what seems to be an "appalling authority" is the past — particularly, her own past. As we have already seen, Del is always eager to learn about any version of the past, and to discard, appropriate, or adapt what she learns for her own purposes. Telling stories is her mother's favourite pastime with Fern Dogherty, their boarder in Jubilee, and for Del their dialogue seems to represent yet another facet of that "real life" that she seeks everywhere but that is always somehow beyond her grasp: "They told stories about people in the town, about themselves; their talk was a river that never dried up. It was the drama, the ferment of life just beyond my reach" (59).

Before recounting her mother's stories, however, Del recalls asking her mother about another kind of rendition of the past — a painting her mother had done years earlier that hangs over the couch in the Flats Road house, now a region increasingly given over to men and boys, to Uncle Benny, Del's father, and Owen. The Flats Road world has begun to recede pastwards in Del's imagination as she enters the world of Jubilee in this chapter, and it is from this perspective that she asks her mother why she doesn't bring the painting into town. Del's initial misapprehension of the meaning and the composition of this painting provides us with an entrance into the wider significance of her insights into the stories her mother will tell her. Del misses the picture because she connects it with her vision of a warmer, more comfortable and benign past, a past in which her mother might have been less harried, when she and her husband might have been young lovers; Del imagines the picture might have been painted "in the far-off early days — the possibly leisured, sunny, loving days — of her marriage" (60). The painting also evokes a past further removed and more directly representational: at one point "Long ago," Del had believed that the girl tending sheep in the picture was actually her mother, and that the landscape was "the desolate country of her early life" (60). Then both conceptions collapsed: she learned that her mother had "copied the scene from the *National Geographic*" (60).

What we see here is Del constructing a story for herself that incorporates an image of her mother that Del longs for, a story that Del has derived, furthermore, from a painting — a painting that she has "read" as a story that her mother is telling about the early days of her marriage. However, Del shows us how she has corrected her vision here, on a deeper level than the corrections she makes to "Uncle" Benny's name on the first page of the novel. She would have liked to believe that the painting told a story showing her mother in guises Del has never seen: as a young and happily married woman with the leisure and inclination to evoke her own past, and as the child evoked in the painting, too. In reality, her mother and father live at a distance from each other most literally depicted in the two houses, but also evoked in their rare physical contact and in the several ways in which their sexuality most often seems to be suppressed or concealed.

In another much-quoted passage from this story, Del recalls how tight a grip her mother kept on the past, and on earlier, clearer incarnations of herself:

> My mother had not let anything go. Inside that self we knew, which might at times appear blurred a bit, or sidetracked, she kept her younger selves strenuous and hopeful; scenes from the past were liable to pop up any time, like lantern slides, against the cluttered fabric of the present. (62)

This passage introduces the major sequence that will replace a more conventional plot, preparing us for Del's mother's stories, for her Uncle Bill's stories, and finally for the insight Del gains into her mother from the discrepancies between her mother's and her Uncle's fictions. Her mother's story (62–68) in which Del's grandmother is the first major character, is one in which poverty, piousness, and cruelty combine to deprive Del's mother of a happier childhood. We are made aware of how intent Del is on recalling the details of her mother's story, and of how aware she is that this is indeed a story, and that she, like her readers, is constructing the story as she records or reads it. In Del's recollection, the story opens with clear signals that it is at once a fairy tale, that it spans a past that reaches back toward geological time spans measured by the birth of rock formations, and that it must stand in place of the kind of record of time that a photograph — like one of Uncle Craig's photographs, for example (24, 25) — might provide her. And it opens, as so many of Del's stories open, with the description of a house; in this novel that traces the birth and growth of an imagination, the house, often very closely described, can be read as a figure for the body that houses the imagination. It is appropriate, then, that with no photograph to rely on, Del should imagine this house, her mother's childhood house, in terms so redolent of gothic horror stories, so suggestive, perhaps, of her mother's evident discomfort within her own body:

> In the beginning, the very beginning of everything, there was that house. It stood at the end of a long lane, with wire fences, sagging windowpanes of wire on either side, in the middle of fields where the rocks — part of the pre-Cambrian Shield — were poking through the soil like bones through flesh. The house which I had never seen in a photograph — perhaps none had ever been taken — and which I had never heard my mother describe except in an impatient, matter-of-fact way ("It was just an old frame house — it never had been painted"), nevertheless appeared in my mind as plainly as if I had seen it in a newspaper — the barest, darkest, tallest of all old frame houses, simple and familiar yet with something terrible about it, enclosing evil, like a house where a murder has been committed. (62–63)

It is apparent in this passage that Del is as much concerned with what she remembers as with how she remembers her mother's story, and this is a focus that will culminate in Del's discussion of how fiction renders the past in "Epilogue: The Photographer." But now, Del remembers her mother's account of her childhood in that house, of how she was cured of religion forever by *her* mother's fanaticism; this strand of the story leads to Del's mother's recollection of the incident involving the inheritance her mother spends on Bibles — a memory that will resurface in the closing scene of this chapter. The story includes Addie's unspecific and therefore all the more suggestive recollection of one brother's cruelty, of his torturing her in the barn; this memory, too, will resurface shortly in an unlikely reincarnation. The story continues with Addie's memories of running away from home after her mother's death, of her time in a boarding-house, of various protectors and mentors in her progress towards an independent life as a teacher. But her progress is arrested, over and again, by a death; death, and attendant treacheries and deceptions, put an end to each episode in her story, until it ends twice: with her marriage to Del's father, and, closer to the narrative present, with the improbable woman Del sees before her eyes, impossible for Del to reconcile with her images of the young girl and young woman in her mother's stories. In other words, the story does not seem to lead coherently to the present. It does not account for her mother; it does not end with love and a conventionally happy marriage. It ends with Del's mother as she is in Jubilee, already losing some of the power that Del had invested in her on the Flats Road. And it ends, disappointingly, with an intimation that alongside the stories they tell, people endure and persist in inexplicably imperfect and ordinary guises, so that Del is left to reflect: "Had all her stories, after all, to end up just with her, the way she was now, just my mother in Jubilee?" (67).

This section of the chapter closes with Del's recollection of her mother in her role as "Princess Ida," writing letters to the newspaper that "made the roots of my teeth ache with shame" (68) because of their flowery and ornate phrasing, their mention of her and of Owen, and above all because of the ways in which Jubilee perceived the letters and their author. Del's strategy in the face of this impossible embarrassment is typical and revelatory, showing us one of the elementary forces that shape her way of being in the world, and showing us, too, how Del's mother serves as an object lesson to her daughter, a model to be admired, but a model whose precepts will need to be acted on in far less explicit ways: "I myself was not so different from my mother, but concealed it, knowing what dangers there were" (68).

The closing section of "Princess Ida" recounts Del's Uncle Bill's visit. His story about his childhood, and his present incarnation as its narrator, become forceful revelations to Del of how her mother's enduring perspective on the past has indeed shaped her character, but not in the straightforward ways that Del had hoped for earlier. As well, Uncle Bill's story is yet another confirmation, reaching from Del's present toward the future, that stories about the past "could go . . . round and round and down to death" (66), in that he is dying of cancer and has come for his last visit to his sister. Two major puzzlements confront Del in her Uncle Bill: first, she cannot find the cruel brother of her mother's stories in him, and it is worth noting that her recounting of this paradox prefaces Uncle Bill's main recollection about his childhood:

> Her brother! This was the thing, the indigestible fact. This Uncle Bill was my mother's brother, the terrible fat boy, so gifted in cruelty, so cunning, quick, fiendish, so much to be feared. I kept looking at him, trying to pull that boy out of the yellowish man. But I could not find him there. He was gone, smothered, like a

little spotted snake, once venomous and sportive, buried in a bag of meal. (74)

The story he tells Del and her mother is of the caterpillar and the cocoon that "Momma" places over the door, where it finally emerges on Easter as a butterfly. It is a gentle story of hope, of patience rewarded by a beautiful transformation and a resurrection, a story that Uncle Bill tells in his own voice, quoted in Del's memory. It so strongly contradicts the climate of feeling created by Addie's stories that at its end, Del closes her narration of it by reflecting: "That was in the same house. The same house where my mother used to find the fire out and her mother at prayer and where she took milk and cucumbers in the hope of getting to heaven" (75). The shocking recognition for Del is not so much that her mother and Uncle Bill have different memories; more, it is the recognition of how the traces of these memories and these stories persist in the storytellers, remaining in a way of seeing, a way of establishing an enduring frame of reference for the past and for the present. Del's mother, as will now become clear to Del, has retained, always close at hand, a grim story of deprivation, of shattered dreams, of hope crushed, of a mother who was " 'a religious fanatic' " (63), and of the hurt she endured as a child and endures still. But Del now sees that this is also her mother's construction of the past — that Uncle Bill, for one, retains and has constructed a story that evokes a very different atmosphere and setting. And it is in the retelling of her mother's story, the reconstruction of it from the many times that her mother, at Del's prodding, has recounted it to her, that Del now constructs her mother's character.

Interestingly, Del's closing insight into her mother's strenuous grip on the past — the clinching evidence that her mother really has not "let anything go" (62) — is narrated as an unexplained, but precisely described perception of Del's in the kitchen with her mother. In reply to Del's question about how she will spend the three hundred dollars that will come to her when Bill dies, her mother remarks: " 'I could always send away for a box of Bibles' " (76), immediately recalling for Del and her readers alike Addie's bitter story about her mother's Bibles. The moment Del then describes stands as her most intense and intimate recognition of her mother's character, a recognition that will signal a crucial shift in their developing relationship:

Just before Fern came in one door and Owen came in the other, there was something in the room like the downflash of a wing or knife, a sense of hurt so strong, but quick and isolated, vanishing. (76)

Addie now deflects attention from her remark and its implication by returning to her crossword puzzle; soon, Del reflects, it will be spring again, and her mother can once again go out on the road selling encyclopedias. But her mother's return to her routines is posed against what Del has learned about her; the patterns of Addie's adult life may continue to recur in predictable, even seasonal cycles, but Del's insights are less predictable and less sequential. What she has learned in the process of retelling her mother's stories leads her inwards towards the contemplation of her own imagination and outwards towards her continuing recollections of her development within her family; but from this point forward, it will be the wider social landscapes of Jubilee that will begin to place much larger demands on her attention. Princess Ida's stories have been retold, and Del has become a more reflective narrator, a more discerning reader, and a less spellbound daughter.

"AGE OF FAITH": WHAT IF GOD WERE REAL?

The cycle of insights that Del gains in the first three chapters teaches her to recognize and accommodate several inexplicable realities: her first intimations of separation from her family, through her insight into Uncle Benny's alternate world; her first encounters with mortality, which, unlike its incarnations in the stories she hears and the lectures she listens to about it, presents itself to her as an unknowable ending; and her early lessons about the ways that stories recreate the past and reveal character — particularly, her mother's character. In "Age of Faith," Del completes her story's opening cycle of insights by recalling her inquiries into the nature and the reality of spiritual belief. Again, Del's curiosity drives her in two related directions — towards a desire to experience the reality she is investigating in her own everyday life, and towards the desire to *imagine* and to *read* the nature of faith through the forms of its social, public manifestations

"Burglars," a draft of the beginning of "Age of Faith."
Special Collections, University of Calgary Libraries.

— in Jubilee's various churches, for example, through the forms of their furnishings and ceremonies, their sermons, liturgies, and imagery. Typically, in this chapter Del will gain, not a confirmation, but a corrective disillusionment, leading to unanswerable questions that she will have to learn both to ask and to accommodate. In fact, in learning to accommodate her unanswerable questions about alternate realities, about mortality, about the stories through which people create their characters and their visions, and now about God and faith, Del is opening herself to a kind of wonderment at reality that will finally compel her to evoke her past over and again, in as many shades and tones as she can recall and imagine.

We have seen how it might be deceptive to construct our reading of the plot of this novel in a straightforward manner, to assume that by following a sequence of major events, causally linked, we will be able to perceive the coherence and the meaning of Del's narration. This assumption might mislead us with "Age of Faith" as well. One alternate way of assembling the details of this chapter into a meaningful sequence might be to pay attention to the transformations in Del's vision of faith, and to notice her points of departure and arrival as her perceptions of faith modulate in the course of her narration.

Before embarking on this interpretative journey, though, it is worth noting how the chapter opens with several of the signals of this book's plural forms. These signals recur at different points throughout *Lives of Girls and Women*, and we are far enough into the book now to see how they operate in this section to allow us to conceive of "Age of Faith" as a chapter, as a self-contained story, and as one of the series of linked stories that comprises the book we are reading. In the opening sentence, the narrator at once assumes that the reader has a certain degree of familiarity with the setting, *and* that the reader needs to be reminded of the setting: "When we lived in that house at the end of the Flats Road, and before my mother knew how to drive a car, she and I used to walk to town; town being Jubilee, a mile away" (77). By referring to "that" house, the narrator seems to assume that we remember "that" house from her description of it in "The Flats Road"; by naming Jubilee as if we were not acquainted with it yet (although we have just had an extended, detailed description of Jubilee in the previous chapter), she seems to be introducing us to a new setting, as if "Age of Faith" were to be a self-contained story. And by explaining that she and her mother used to walk to town before her mother knew how to drive, Del seems to be placing these events before the events recalled in "Princess Ida," with its opening description of Del's mother driving "over all of the highways and back roads of Wawanash County" (55), so that the chronology of the chapters is not always sequential, as we might expect it to be were the book clearly and exclusively a novel. Of course, this question of chronology is further complicated throughout the book by the ways in which Del ranges freely over the past within each section, so that in "Age of Faith," for example, it is never immediately clear how much time elapses between Del's first conception of the burglars her mother believes in, and Del's later re-evaluation of this conception (77–78).

Two other points about "Age of Faith" are worth mentioning here. First, it is, interestingly enough, the least sombre and the most comic of the book's chapters. This may not seem so striking until we compare its treatment of the question of faith with other fictional explorations of the same issue in contemporary Canadian writing, and with Del's mother's grimmer perspective on her own mother and her Bibles. Think, for example, of Robertson Davies's *Fifth Business* and Dunstan Ramsay's lifelong quest, and its similar original setting in small-town Ontario; early in *Fifth Business*, in fact, Ramsay catalogues the differences between the five churches in Deptford in ways that might seem, both in tone and content, to recall Del's more extended descriptions of Jubilee's churches (78–79).[14] The point is that Del's exploration of the question becomes somewhat comical because of the perspective she adopts — a perspective that opens with her admission that she "had never had a picture of God so clear and uncomplicated as my picture of the burglars" (78). This assertion affirms both Del's awareness of the naïveté of her earlier conception of burglars and the shift to more momentous matters, but the transition also establishes a somewhat comical linkage between these two conceptions, recalling the ironic tone of Del's admission, a few lines earlier, that as a child she believed that "Our world was steadfastly reflected in burglar minds" (78). "Age of Faith" is the one chapter in *Lives of Girls and Women*, perhaps, in which the wry, gentle irony of the older narrator looking back over her younger self's perceptions tends to obscure or to undercut her younger incarnations, so that childlike conceptions threaten at times to seem merely childish.

The second point follows from the first. Although Del treats the issue of faith with gentle irony for much of the chapter, her tone changes quite dramatically towards the end of this section when Major is to be destroyed for killing sheep and Owen is desperate for Del to teach him how to pray. "Age of Faith" is arguably the weakest section of *Lives of Girls and Women* because the urgency of Del's quest for God — the seriousness and energy with which she recalls herself having searched as a girl for tangible signs, proofs of His power or presence — is undercut at times by the gentle irony and comedy that she conveys through her perspective as she looks back on this "age." And yet if this is really a weakness, it may be an instructive one. Del's acceptance of the mystery of faith as a reality not to be encountered or understood within the socially sanctioned rituals of the church helps to further clarify the divergences between Del and her mother, a determined atheist who rejects the idea of a God wherever it might be proposed, and, perhaps, to resonate within our reading of her relationship with Garnet French in "Baptizing" — a relationship embedded in several ways within the context of ironic references to rituals of salvation.

Del's progress in "Age of Faith" can be read as two parallel series of false confirmations, followed by two disillusionments that produce two related questions in Del's mind about the nature of God and faith. The first series of episodes traces Del's search for God in her everyday life, in her school life, and her family life, and its high point is Del's alleged success in praying to God to intercede on her behalf in her Household Science class, so that she does not have to fail yet again at threading the sewing machine. In this series of episodes, her arguments over the existence of God take the form of debates with her mother and with Owen, who is at first oblivious to her entreaties. These episodes culminate in the incident involving Major, the family dog, and his killing the neighbour's sheep out on the Flats Road, leading to her father's resolve to shoot Major, to Owen's desperate attempts to pray for intervention, and to Del's perception of the sometimes murderous and yet eminently reasonable intentions of adults — even of her father. In something of the same way as the incident with the cow in "Heirs of the Living Body" prepares Del and her readers for her responses to Uncle Craig's death (and, eventually, to the death of his history of Wawanash County), this series of incidents in "Age of Faith" frames the more imaginative, more central, and more vital series of episodes involving Del's search for God within the church. Her arguments in these episodes are internalized, and they culminate in her more perplexing doubts, listening to the Anglican Minister's Good Friday sermon, about how Christ on the cross might have understood his faith (91–92). It is as if Del has on one level taken to heart her mother's stance regarding God and faith; but then, because she has an imagination that will not allow for the kind of determined reliance on *explanation* that informs her mother's character so thoroughly, Del's internal argument with the Minister leads her to an unanswerable, and yet eloquently formulated question about God's presence. The passage recording this question, like several others in this chapter, is set off typographically both to illustrate its importance and, perhaps, to enshrine it as one of the texts central to Del's story, another unanswerable but vital question, important precisely because she has succeeded in formulating it, so that its very articulation signals its enduring significance:

Could there be God not contained in the churches' net at all, not made manageable by any spells and crosses, God real, and really in the world, and alien and unacceptable as death? Could there be God amazing, indifferent, beyond faith? (96)

The passage is a striking one in several ways. It reminds us of Del's life-long, Munro's book-long preoccupation with the "real"; we might recall the novel's first title, the last words of "Baptizing" ("Real Life"), and, in this chapter, Del's related and recurrent puzzlement over in what sense, if any, the story of Christ could be "true," and the further, perhaps inevitable question of how this story should be believed. We might be reminded as well of Del's earlier encounter with mortality, which she discovers is also "really real," and her attempts to understand death; now she asks whether God, like death, is not another "alien, unacceptable" presence. And first and last, the passage calls attention to the significance of Munro's style: "amazing, indifferent," for example, are adjectives that signal the complexity of Del's vision, a vision that not only reconciles opposites and resolves paradoxes (a relatively simple binary operation), but that also allows abstractions to assume tangible forms, as if they were the particular, named elements of everyday life, no more portentous, and yet just as portentous, as the "kitchen linoleum" Del evokes to describe the surfaces and the depths of people's lives in the closing section (210).

It is important to consider how Del has arrived at this question, as distinct from the way in which she arrives at the question that closes the chapter: "Do missionaries ever have these times, of astonishment and shame?" (97). That question frames Del's wry acknowledgement of her inability to comfort Owen, of her own disbelief in the kind of faith that would save Major from her father, that would change the course of events psychologically, sociologically fore-ordained because of the ways in which adults behave in a world governed by laws Del is just discovering. The operations of naked faith seen close at hand, Del discovers through Owen's attempts at prayer, are no more easier to look at than "seeing someone chop a finger off" (97).

The chapter's closing question is posed in the voice we now recognize as one variant of Del's older voice, of Del the young woman speaking as she looks back on Del the girl.

But the question about God's possible place in the world is posed in the style and the language that conjure the writer's imagination at work, and that draw their resonances from Del's engagement with what she calls the "theatrical" elements in religion (83). She is referring to all of the forms and rituals that so "strongly delighted" her in the Anglican service (83); she savours the bare dignity of the "poverty, smallness, shabbiness" of the church, and she relishes the power of language in its triumph over this scant setting: "The richness of the words against the poverty of the place" (83). In effect, she is enraptured with this *rendition* of faith, just as in "Princess Ida" she was enchanted with the history presented to her in the sumptuous pages of the encyclopedia; and her final disillusionment with the "theatrical" form of the liturgy as she listens to the sermon and questions its assumptions leads directly to her question about the possible presence of God outside of the churches' net — His presence, perhaps, "really real," not as an all-powerful, abstract entity, but as a vital sign of the operations of her imagination.

At the end of "Age of Faith," Del has reached a temporary point of equilibrium, looking back over various ends to childhood, over certainties revealed to be mysteries, over the failure even of knowledge to provide her with a bulwark against death, or against the unpredictably volatile, tender, brutal, unaccountable adult world she glimpses from a safe but tantalizing distance. The next cycle of stories will take Del more directly into the ambiguities, dreams, and desires arising from her imagination as it turns to her own sexuality, to the life and the story of her body.

"CHANGES AND CEREMONIES": THE OPERETTA OF LOVE

In the four chapters we have looked at so far, Del has taken us back through several of the major episodes that define her experience as a young girl, reassessing, correcting, and revising her recollections with the insights she gains through her narration, through remembering and writing about these episodes. The narrator of "Changes and Ceremonies," more clearly than the Del Jordan we know from earlier in the novel, is beginning to gain insights that are teaching her about both her life and her art. For our part, we may become more aware that we are reading two complementary and evolving stories. The stories Del tells in this chapter are about the beginnings of her exploration of love and sexuality, but they are also about the relations, as well as the differences, between life and art.

We can begin to see the signs of these stories' evolutions in the chapter's opening sentence: "Boys' hate was dangerous, it was keen and bright, a miraculous birthright, like Arthur's sword snatched out of the stone, in the Grade Seven Reader" (98). This perception signals the beginning of the thematic shift that will take us through the next four chapters to the "Epilogue," as Del imagines and experiences several kinds of love and sexuality. Just as significantly, though, the style of the sentence invites us, as so much of Del's narration does, to imagine her evolving formulation of the relations between life and art; this formulation will develop later into her insights into the connections between her life in Jubilee and her own art as a writer. Del opens the sentence by transcribing her everyday experience of boys' hate through a series of adjectives that describe its qualities, "dangerous," "keen," "bright"; the "miraculous birthright" that follows, however, leads us through the simile Del creates — "like Arthur's sword snatched out of the stone" — to the figurative realm of *literary* experience that Del draws on throughout *Lives of Girls and Women* to interpret her life. Here, the allusion is one that Del calls up from her Grade Seven Reader, establishing the importance in this chapter of what Del reads, and of how she draws on her reading to explain her life.

In terms of the overarching shape of *Lives of Girls and Women*, this relation between literal and literary experience is an important element in understanding Del's development as a writer; in this chapter, the relation is more specific, because in "Changes and Ceremonies" Del provides her first sustained exploration of how art and life both do and do not reflect each other — and of how art both teaches and does not teach her about life. She does this in the context of what we might call, if Del were a storyteller less aware of the form, more concerned with the content of her experience, simply an exploration of first love. But Del remembers her first experience of love primarily within the setting of Miss Farris's operetta and its production, and this context has implications that resonate beyond the literal and personal dimensions of Del's life to qualify our understanding of the development of her sensibility and imagination.

It is important to notice how Del leads us to the chapter's major focus on the operetta, on Miss Farris, and on Del's love for Frank Wales. The opening reports first on boys' hate, and then on what boys say to girls, drawing our attention once again to the power, in this case the tyranny, of language. The boys' freedom to *say* "anything" (98), which Del recalls with careful attention to *how* the boys speak (they say things "softly" or in "tones of cheerful disgust") is, paradoxically, precisely the liberty that takes away the girls' freedom to *be* "what you wanted" (98). This element of her social world, then, is one that begins to imprison Del and her friend Naomi in gender roles defined by what others say, particularly, what boys say (and what they imagine) about sexual roles, sexual identities, and female genitals — about girls' and women's bodies. The girls are "hooers" (the eccentric orthography, presumably a transcription of what the boys *say*, might at once indicate their derisive tone and a contempt that masks secret curiosity and desire, in ways related to Del's "luscious" expansion of "Day-ud cow" [37]); and the boys attempt to demystify the vagina, wherever it is, by naming it a "fuckhole" (98). The boys in Jubilee are just as curious and mystified about sexuality as the girls; but their curiosity manifests itself as aggression, while the girls, conforming with social codes, respond with a different kind of hate that seems to Del to be "muddled and tearful, sourly defensive" (98). One consequence of this oppression — and we are invited to establish this causal relation by the sequence of Del's narration — might be to drive Del into the world of books, lying "alongside" her social world as Uncle Benny's world did earlier.

From the opening description of boys' and girls' hate, Del moves to an extended description of the pleasure she takes in reading. In several ways, the text we read alerts us to Del's own familiarity with words: on the way to the library with her friend Naomi, Del sees the letters that announce the LAD ES REST RO M and the PUBL C RE DING ROOM, remarking that because everyone "had learned to read the words without them," the "missing letters were never replaced" (98). The effect of reproducing the words with spaces for the missing letters is intriguing; it seems at one level to affirm, as so many other kinds of details do in the novel, the verisimilitude of Del's account, confirming our feeling that we are reading a story about a real place, a "true" place, because of what seems so obviously an accurate rendition of setting. At the same time, this passage, like others we have noted throughout — Benny's newspaper headlines, for one — foregrounds Del's awareness of words and of texts. In this case, the text is commonplace — so easily understood that even missing letters will not affect anyone's reading.

The library is presided over by Bella Phippen, "deaf as a stone and lame in one leg from polio," a woman who has been made librarian because she could not hold down a "proper job" (99). If we are moved to interpret characters in *Lives of Girls and Women* as individual incarnations of Jubilee's social norms, Bella Phippen is a good place to start: it would appear as if the importance that Jubilee ascribes to reading, and to the library, is reflected in the town's assessment of the qualifications necessary for her job. And it is fitting that she passes her time as she does, making Kewpie dolls, all identical, which she gives "to every girl who got married in Jubilee" (99). It is tempting to read Del's description of Bella Phippen's dolls as a comment on the fate awaiting marriageable Jubilee girls, a fate Del will watch Naomi willingly engage.

Del's recollections of the library are richly detailed, and they begin with her extended catalogue of the books themselves — their titles, but also, in ways reminiscent of Del's description of her mother's encyclopedias, with close descriptions of the books' appearance, and with quotations from their texts:

> They were old, dull blue and green and brown books with slightly softened, slightly loosened, covers. They would often have a frontispiece showing a pale watercolored lady in some sort of Gainsborough costume, and underneath some such words as these: *Lady Dorothy sought seclusion in the rose garden,*

the better to ponder the import of this mysterious communication. (p. 112) (99)

This is a good example of one of the ways in which *Lives of Girls and Women*, like much contemporary fiction, invites us to contemplate the nature of the book we are reading. By showing us this description of Del's, evoking the books Del reads and her responses to them, this passage establishes one of the many lines of connection between Del's reading and Del's life, and, by extension, a connection between *our* reading of this fiction and the ways in which we interpret our own experience. Within *Lives of Girls and Women* as a whole, this connection will lead us towards Del's own conception of fiction and of her purpose as a writer; but in this section, passages like this one begin to anticipate more specifically this chapter's major depiction of the art form Del plays a role in, the operetta.

Del lingers over her descriptions of the books in the library; if she has just recently established her first friendship with a peer (Naomi is mentioned briefly in "Age of Faith," but Del's first exploration of their friendship is in "Changes and Ceremonies"), she makes it clear that her longer lasting relationships have been with these books, these "Lovely, wistful, shabby old friends" (99), some of which she doesn't read any more. There are also books she has never touched but that she describes as if the books were human bodies, texts that she "knew so well by their spines, knew the curve of every letter in their titles" (99). In a simile that takes us from the realm of books into the public, social world of Jubilee, Del reverses the direction that we followed in the chapter's opening sentence: the books, she recalls, "were like people you saw on the street day after day, year after year, but never knew more than their faces; this could happen even in Jubilee" (99).

But "Changes and Ceremonies," as the title implies, is also about transformations, and one of these involves Del's gradual relinquishing of her books, or at least, of the kinds of books she has been reading in the town library. This development runs in a rough parallel with the evolution of her friendship with Naomi, who has a more typical Jubilee attitude than Del does towards reading. Del attempts to mollify Naomi by finding her books that deal with various aspects of sexuality. But the extended description of childbirth in *Kristin Lavransdatter* ("... Kristin has her first baby, hour after hour, page after page, blood and agony, squatting on the straw" in Del's transcription

[100]) only serves to confirm Naomi's received wisdom that if a girl " 'has to get married, she either dies having it, or she nearly dies, or else there is something the matter with it' " (100). Naomi, less trusting of what she reads in novels, is more accepting than Del of what she hears in the world. She claims to have received her information about childbirth from her mother, a nurse, but this source proves just as unreliable as, if not more luridly melodramatic than, *Kristin Lavransdatter*. In fact, throughout this novel, mothers' attitudes towards their daughters' sexuality is presented as imperviously practical, distant but invasive, and generally, singularly unhelpful; and this attitude will be echoed later in Jerry Storey's widowed mother, who acts both as a sister to her son and as a birth control counsellor to Del (167-68). This is one reason for the girls' mystification about sexuality, and for Del's recurring search for explanations.[15]

Del's friendship with Naomi leads her and her readers out of one world of romance — the world in which sexuality is evoked in novels like *Kristin Lavransdatter* — into two alternate worlds: the social realities of the classroom and of Jubilee, and, more importantly, the world Miss Farris creates in the operetta. But here and throughout the novel, Del shows us that her relationship with Naomi is both a liberation and a prison. It is a social alliance through which Del can assume a public identity, and share information and secrets about boyfriends and about the mysteries of sex; but it is also a friendship which in Del's memory will begin to trace Naomi's life as a kind of object lesson, a cautionary tale about growing up and spending her life in Jubilee in accordance with Jubilee norms.

The other, and more central cautionary story of a Jubilee life and death, though — the life and death of a girl/woman — is the one about Miss Farris. Del's first description of Miss Farris not only anticipates Miss Farris's central role in directing and staging the operetta, but also, in ways less mystifying for us than for Del, the more tragic and predictable end of Miss Farris's real life. She has always lived in Jubilee, and gone to the same school Del now goes to; but she has not passed through the same necessary stages that Del is recalling in her life. Although she is a teacher, Miss Farris's first name, Elinor, is "well known" (102), one of the many signs that she seems to be arrested at one level in a perpetual girlhood, although Del makes it clear that she "was not young, either," despite her girlish skating costumes. She makes all her own clothes, and lives "in her own little house," which Del describes in terms that make the cheery veneer and the fairy-tale artifice of Miss Farris's life painfully apparent (106). Jubilee gossip to the contrary, Miss Farris does not seem to Del to be trying to "catch a man," as Fern Dogherty puts it, or to be romantically involved with Mr. Boyce, the music teacher (102). In Del's eyes, as she reads Miss Farris's face ("self-consciously rouged and animated, with flickering commas at the corners of her mouth, bright startled eyes" [103]), Miss Farris's sexuality seems to be more ambiguously sublimated: "Whatever she was after, it could not be Mr. Boyce. Fern Dogherty notwithstanding, it could hardly even be men" (103).

What Miss Farris is really after is largely unattainable in that it resides largely as an ideal — a perfect recreation of life and love in art, standing in, perhaps, for the missing elements in her impoverished existence beyond the confines of the stage. What animates Miss Farris's whole life are the six operettas that she directs and produces. The parts that her charges play in them, male and female, are more real to her than their roles in the world; the 1937 captain of *The Gypsy Princess*, Pierce Murray, is later killed in the air force, but it is his way of swinging the cloak he wore in the operetta that Miss Farris recalls (109). In Del's memory Miss Farris vibrates with a dangerous, tiny hum of energy that Del senses as Miss Farris gets caught up in staging the operetta; it is as if Miss Farris gives off a crystallized, safe version of the sexuality that, let loose or encountered at large in the world, might be just as volatile and threatening as Del's idea of God in "Age of Faith." In fact, when Naomi instructs Del about the reasons that boys can't control their sexual impulses, cannot be held responsible for them, and explains that girls can do both, since unlike boys', girls' sexual organs are "on the inside" (112), Del reflects that Naomi's tone of voice "acknowledged the anarchy, the mysterious brutality prevalent in that adjacent world" (112), in a passage that also recalls Del's opening vision of Uncle Benny's world lying "alongside" her own within her family.

It is within the artificial confines of the operetta — "The Pied Piper" — and the roles that the boys and girls assume for it, that Del discovers her love for Frank Wales. We should note that in the everyday world of the classroom, Frank is only an average boy (although he is an atrocious speller). It is only within the exalted, theatrical confines of the operetta, in its enclosed structure and space, with its well-formed story, with laws and procedures, manners and morals all regulated, all directed and supervised, all orchestrated so that there is no mystifying gap between appearance and reality, that Del can safely fall in love with Frank Wales. The obligatory hatred between the sexes can be suspended; this is only an act. But the relations between art and life, operetta and classroom are more ambiguous and more complex than this simple opposition might suggest; more accurately, and more in keeping with the vision that Del is fostering, they are worlds that lie "alongside" each other, that interpenetrate. Del will not make the fatal mistake that Miss Farris does, of being forced to believe wholly only in one of them, and to live as if it were the laws of the world of the operettas that would order her life. As she recalls, "I loved him. I loved the Pied Piper. I loved Frank Wales" (110); she can love both Frank Wales, the character in the operetta, and by extension, Frank Wales, her classmate, soon to leave school for the working world. When Frank Wales assumes the role of the Pied Piper, Del thinks that she is able to see his true character emerge for the first time, as if the stage, and his role in the operetta, and the way in which he interpreted the part, accentuated what his essence was and allowed her to perceive it (110). The operetta might be seen, then, to function as a testing-ground for Del, a staging area for her to try on her fantasies, to allow herself to perceive another person in a more complete incarnation than she would allow herself, or be allowed, in the more anarchic, random, dangerous world offstage.

For Miss Farris, however, migrations between art and life are not so easy. Even Mr. Boyce's signal of approval, his dramatic "*Con Brio*, Miss Farris!" on discovering her making a "swashbuckling swing" for the girls in the Teachers' Room (109) as she imitates Pierce Murray's gestures, suggests that she transposes the stage more fully onto the world at large, where she continues to perform her dry, cheery, orphaned schoolgirl's part (her assumption of Pierce Murray's pose and role at this point is, perhaps, another sign of her confused sexual identity). Del and Naomi can imagine themselves in love with Frank Wales and Dale McLaughlin, and also hope that after the operetta, the boys will walk them home; Miss Farris can only orchestrate the conditions that will allow her students these latitudes, while her own more vicarious satisfaction expires immediately upon the operetta's conclusion. Del recalls that after the performance, Miss

Farris's "chest actually looked concave, as if something had collapsed inside it" (116).

Following the staging of the operetta, Del and her classmates return, with some relief, to their routines. But Del recognizes that she has returned to a reality in which another set of perceptions has been corrected: one comical sign of this in the classroom is the janitor's removal of an old sock, long thought to be a condom, from one of the hanging lights. As Del reflects in an observation that takes in more territory than this episode, it "seemed to be a time for dispelling illusions" (117). The aura of brutality, mystery, and danger surrounding sexuality has begun to disperse, and the romantic and melodramatic veils suspended over love have also begun to lift. Even the change of season from winter to spring helps to reveal the ordinary aspects of Jubilee and the surrounding countryside; Del conceives of winter as an enclosing season in which, as in the operetta, "fantastic hopes might bloom" (117), so that it is winter, and not spring, that seemed to her to be the season for love. But this illusion, as well, has been dispelled in the very process of identifying it.

Reality intervenes in other, more predictable ways to dispel what Del now calls her "daydreams" as Frank Wales leaves high school and goes to work for Jubilee Dry Cleaners. It takes Del some six months' time to grow out of her attraction to Frank Wales, but it is "three or four years" later that Miss Farris dies, when Del is already in high school. The passages describing Miss Farris's death take us through Del's process of accommodating the event, beginning with the passive construction, "Miss Farris was drowned in the Wawanash River" (117), with its ambiguous implications concerning the nature of her death.

The chapter's closing is striking in several respects. Beyond the ways in which Miss Farris's death relates to Del's education in this chapter, we might see in her drowning echoes of other deaths and other escapes: Marion Sherriff's suicide in the Wawanash, which becomes one of the catalysts for the novel Del conceives in the "Epilogue," and Del's own escape from Garnet French's attempt to "baptize" her in the river during their final confrontation (196–99). Because of these resonances, we might suppose with hindsight that the Wawanash functions as a kind of ironic baptismal font — a river that, while it might provide generously for Uncle Benny in his alternate world, supplying him both with fish and sustenance for his store of tales about the surrounding swampland, receives into its (quite shallow) depths the lost, the disgraced, and the desperate from Jubilee. Del's escape from Garnet in the river, then, gains an additional significance.

More importantly, Miss Farris's death — which Del, like the majority of people in Jubilee, finally concludes is a suicide — presents her with a final image in a series that she cannot accommodate along with her other snapshot memories of Miss Farris. The chapter begins to close with Del's attempt to range these images alongside each other, as if each were an alternate world, with the final one altering the whole series:

> Miss Farris in her velvet skating costume, her jaunty fur hat bobbing among the skaters, always marking her out, Miss Farris *con brio*, Miss Farris painting faces in the Council Chambers, Miss Farris floating face down, unprotesting, in the Wawanash River, six days before she was found. Though there is no plausible way of hanging those pictures together — if the last one is true then must it not alter the others? — they are going to have to stay together now. (118)

The last image must, indeed, alter the others, because Del's understanding of her past, unlike the "transformed childish selves" trapped forever in Miss Farris's operetta, along with her own "undefeated," but also fatally "unrequited" love (118), changes during the course of her recollections, during the course of her narration.

The closing paragraph of the chapter, with its half amused glance at Mr. Boyce in his new life in London, Ontario (and its wry concession to the novel's American readers, explaining that this London is in Canada), removes us for a moment from the sobering insight that Del is on the verge of gaining from her assembly of "pictures." But the force of the accommodation Del must now make stays with us. The "Changes" and the "Ceremonies" invoked in the chapter's title, we might now conclude, have been working throughout this section on several levels. Del changes as a result of the ceremonies of the operetta, of her friendship with Naomi, of the daily rituals in school and Jubilee, learning some first lessons about love and sexuality, and learning, as well, about Miss Farris's desolately cheerful ceremonies and their end. But it might also be true that she learns about change through another kind of ceremony: Del changes the course of her life by following the changing course of her memories, and she renders all of these changes through the most vital ceremony of all, the ceremony of narration that so mysteriously clarifies her story.

"LIVES OF GIRLS AND WOMEN": A PHALLIC STORY UNTOLD

In "Changes and Ceremonies," Del's daydream of love for Frank Wales fades after the operetta. But her curiosity about sexuality — despite the descriptions in the novels she reads in the library, the information imparted by Naomi and her mother, and the classroom stories that circulate about Dale McLaughlin and Alma Cody — remains a strong undercurrent in her imagination. Sexuality is still a text that needs to be interpreted, that does not inform her awareness of her own body or desires as much as it seems to Del to reside beyond her, at a slight remove in the world, on the stage, or in her mind. In the novel's title story, Del encounters male sexual expression (and oppression) in a new and more direct guise, in a disillusioning but instructive performance that reforms her desires, sexual as well as psychological, social as well as artistic.

Del is now in her first year of high school, where her friendship with Naomi has entered a phase of adolescent rebellious play, of simulating fits on the street or hanging upside down from trees in the park. Their relationship is strengthened most, though, by their mutual determination to find out about sex, whether it be from Naomi's mother's book, with its clinical descriptions of intercourse and its reports on the size of the erect male sexual organ (123), or through their speculations about Fern Dogherty's relations with Art Chamberlain, the newscaster on Jubilee's radio station.

Significantly, Del meets Chamberlain first in her mother's house, the setting for the other sphere of relationships in this chapter. The house is the locus for Del's mother's and Fern's long talks, as we saw first in "Princess Ida"; now it will also be the point of departure and return for Del in her first encounter with male sexuality. The clandestine nature of this experience is anticipated in the undisclosed relationship between Fern and Art Chamberlain, unconsciously sanctioned by Del's mother. In fact, in a further suggestion of relationship, if not complicity, the house Del's family lives in is rented from Chamberlain's "blind and bedridden" mother, who, like Fern's mother, lives in the Wawanash County Hospital (122). It is almost as if Fern and Chamberlain, under her mother's (rented) roof, act as surrogate parents and partners who present Del with an illegitimate, unsanctioned, alluring version of "connection," an alternate version of the story of her mother's and father's marriage, with its partners living apart and inhabiting such different worlds and such different houses.

Del's quest for sexual knowledge and experience is complemented by her powerfully felt, if unspecified drive for "glory," as she describes it in a passage that might be seen as faintly echoing the famous Joycean prescription for an artist's conduct ("silence, exile, and cunning"[16]). The faintly ironic ring in Del's tone is not directed at the reality or strength of her conviction at that age; rather, it is a sign of Del the writer's more distanced and insightful perspective on herself:

> It was glory I was after, walking the streets of Jubilee like an exile or a spy, not sure from which direction fame would strike, or when, only convinced from my bones out that it had to. (119–20)

The structure of the chapter is outlined by the seasonal change from winter to spring, reminiscent of the shape of "Changes and Ceremonies." More ironically, the chapter is also framed by Del's mother's opening and closing predictions and lectures. The chapter begins with a description of Jubilee in midwinter and of a photograph of the arch cut in the abnormally high snowbank in front of the post office (119); Del's mother saves the picture from the town newspaper because it has Fern in it, and because Del will be able to show it to her children, her mother tells her. She goes on to explain to Del that in the future, technology will in effect do away with seasons, that " 'snow will all be collected in machines and — dissipated' " (119). Del's response links her amusement at her mother's predictions about the future with her incredulity at her mother's assumption that Del will have children: "Her speaking of my children amazed me too, for I never meant to have any" (119). Her mother, we might infer, is as wrong about the future of natural, seasonal cycles as she is about her daughter's nature and intentions — as if, like sexuality, nature in Del's mother's worldview could be controlled, protected against, or perhaps regulated out of mind. If technology can perfect the kinds of prophylactics that Del's mother, to Del's embarrassment, advocates distributing to all women on relief in Wawanash County (147), then it might follow that technology will also devise systems for circumventing seasonal cycles on a wider scale.

Del's mother's perspective is undercut in several ways by the development of the story that unfolds in her domain. As winter gives way to spring, Del's sexuality urges her into a natural world that she will perceive and describe, within Art Chamberlain's realm of influence, as "debased, maddeningly erotic" (140); and in the scene that closes the chapter, as Del sits with her mother on the steps, the developing distance between her mother's and her own vision and experience is sharply evoked. Del has been reading about sex in the modern novels that her mother deplores for their depictions of bodily functions (we might think again of Joyce, and of the long scene near the beginning of *Ulysses* in which Leopold Bloom is sitting in the outhouse[17]). Del's mother complains, " 'Next day they will be telling about how they go to the toilet, why do they leave that out?' " (145). But Del has concluded, in a perception that anticipates her sexual (and, in large part, wordless) relationship with Garnet French, that "Books always compared it to something else, never told about it by itself" (146).

Her mother doesn't want Del to read; she wants her company on the steps, Del perceives. Her mother invites Del to contemplate the change of season, but her real purpose in talking to Del emerges quickly: it is to use Fern as an object lesson to instruct Del about how women can be entrapped by men, and then to open out her instruction into her famous prophecy about the " 'change coming ... in the lives of girls and women' " (146). The irony here works on several levels. First, we might notice the symmetry of the chapter's opening and ending: each of Del's mother's lectures closes with her observation that Del will have children, followed by Del's rejection of this assumption. At the end of the chapter, Del's mother sees Del's having children as a reality that will have to be accommodated despite her warning to Del about how men regard women — a warning that draws on Tennyson, one of "Princess Ida's" favoured sources, we recall, and that ends with her assumption, presented as an accepted truth: " 'You will want to have children, though' " (147). Del's silent response — "That was how much she knew me" — recalls her response to this same assumption at the opening of the chapter and reflects the constancy of her mother's expectations and of Del's own resolve, which has been strengthened by her experience with Art Chamberlain.

The story of Del's encounters with Mr. Chamberlain develops on several levels, reflecting Del's characteristic attempts to anticipate, explain, or resolve her experience through fiction-making; but this is a process that she discovers she does not want to use this time, with this experience. The world that Del inhabits has become saturated with hints, stories, texts, and gestures that intimate sexuality, but that she cannot enter herself. Instead, she finds herself in the role of an observer confronted with a spectacle, culminating, of course, in the scene in which Art Chamberlain masturbates in front of her. If we follow the ways in which Del's narration leads us to this scene, we find her exploring sexual lore in her attempts to accommodate this element of her experience of her own body with her perceptions of the ordinary, everyday world — the world of kitchen linoleum that somehow contains, not only mortality and a possibly alien or indifferent God, but, closer to home, the unimaginable, perhaps violent, possibly ecstatic reality of sexual communication.

Del sees Fern Dogherty, in explicit contrast with her own mother, as a woman whose appearance embodies the possibilities of sexuality, mentioning her skin and her teeth, which she describes in detail, as the "two characteristics, neither of which sounds particularly attractive in itself, [that] did give her a roguish, sensual look" (120). She closely describes Fern's clothing, which in its contours suggests to Del Fern's comfort and accommodation with her own body and sexuality: "She had a ruby-colored satin dressing gown, a gorgeous garment, fruitily molding, when she sat down, the bulges of her stomach and thighs" (120). The description renders Fern as a renaissance painting of a woman in recline, her clothes serving not to cover, but to reveal her ample, generous proportions, "fruitily molding" her shape. Del's own body is more foreign territory, so much so that she cannot bear to wear a nightgown since it leaves her "uncovered between the legs," so that she cannot help but be aware of her "vile bundle" (a description as distanced and distancing in its way as the boys' "fuckhole" [98]), which pajamas like the ones her mother wears can "decently shroud and contain" (120).

If Del's description of Fern Dogherty speaks richly of Del's perceptions of Fern's sexuality, her description of Art Chamberlain is more ambiguous. He has a "fine professional voice," as befits a radio announcer, but that also signals his talents for speaking in many different registers, as Del will soon hear. Fern, too, has a remarkable voice, having once trained to be an opera singer. But she has given this up, so that now her singing becomes another incarnation to Del of the unbridgeable gap between the mundane and the mysterious, between everyday reality and what it might conceal: "The force, the seriousness of her singing voice always came as a surprise. It didn't embarrass her, letting loose those grand, inflated emotions she paid no attention to in life" (121).

To Del, Mr. Chamberlain's clothes also seem to conform to his body, but not in the way Fern's clothes relate to hers. Fern's gown makes her body more apparent; Mr. Chamberlain's body "did not in any way disturb his clothes but seemed to be made of the same material as they were"; this aspect and others of his appearance, recalls Del, "were strange to me in a man" (124), and suggest the motif of concealment or disguise that is an important facet of Mr. Chamberlain's character and that prefigures his eventual unmasking of his real intentions. In a comment that at first might seem paradoxical, Del then notes that Mr. Chamberlain is missing one of the elements that characterizes men for her, and that we have already seen suggested in some of her descriptions and recollections of her father — "some look or way of moving that predicted chance or intended violence, something that would make disorder" (124–25). But it is Mr. Chamberlain who has in fact participated in institutionalized violence, in the war; and he tells stories that make war and killing into a kind of play, telling Del, her mother and father, and Fern about incinerating an Allied tank by mistake, and about blowing up the cookhouse on the last day of the war (125).

From his recollections of the war, Mr. Chamberlain's stories modulate to his memories of Italy; for Del's mother, this must be the Italy she knows, rich with history, treasury of art. But when she brings in an encyclopedia picture of Michelangelo's David, Mr. Chamberlain does not remember seeing it, although Del, in a moment of complicity with Fern (and, perhaps, with Mr. Chamberlain) marvels at her mother's "staunch and dreadful innocence," showing an image of a naked man to them all, while Fern fights off the urge to smile (126).

Mr. Chamberlain's own memories of Italy, of a father trying to " 'sell ... his own daughter,' " a girl " 'No older than Del here' " (126–27), carry within them the possibilities Del has been circling and precipitate Del's first sexual fantasy involving Mr. Chamberlain. Upstairs, she plays at being the object of Mr. Chamberlain's desire, a figure composed at once of the Italian girl, of Del's mother, and of Fern. She dresses in her mother's "black rayon dressing gown" — reminiscent of Fern's "gorgeous garment," and an "impractical gift" that her mother "never wore" (127) — and imagines herself a girl in Italy, feeling seduced first by the sound of Mr. Chamberlain's voice, which felt "like the touch of rayon silk on my skin" (so that his voice becomes a kind of voluptuous clothing), making her feel "endangered and desired" (127). Anticipating Mr. Chamberlain's eventual performance, she fantasizes about what happens next between male and female: "Did he take down his pants or did he simply unzip himself and point his thing at you?" (127). But this fantasy, like most of Del's conceptions in this chapter, brings her to an impasse, because she cannot imagine the connection between people's everyday appearances and their transformations into sexual beings: "It was the stage of transition, bridge between what was possible, known and normal behaviour, and the magical, bestial act, that I could not imagine" (127).

In the midst of her description of this fantasy, and in another demonstration of the practical, literalist impulse that continues to be a powerful element in her imagination, Del describes walking past Jubilee's whorehouse, trying to imagine how one of the women she sees sitting in the yard and reading the newspaper could possibly be the same woman who is reputed to have "been persuaded to serve a line-up, standing up," in the men's toilet at the Gay-la dance hall (127–28). But again, her imagination cannot make this connection.

The next phase in Del's pursuit of her pursuer is to construct a story like a "daydream," in which she arranges a seduction scene in the house, having disposed of her mother, Owen, and Fern in plausible ways. In this story, it is Del who acts while Mr. Chamberlain resides in a "corner" of her story as she arranges the circumstances for her revealing herself naked to him. But Del finds that she cannot go beyond this point, even in her daydream: it is as if her imagination can only reflect her experience — including her reading experience — and since it is she herself, as well as what she has read, that now stands at the centre of the story, she cannot go further than the point at which what is known, or at least visible to her — her own body — is revealed. As we will see, reality will only serve in this chapter to confirm what her imagination gives to her as this unbridgeable gap.

One mystery concealed beneath the surface of everyday life, or on the other side of this gap, is the phallus, and another progression that we can follow is Del's various depictions and conceptions of the phallus. The subtitle for this chapter is intended to indicate what I take to be the purpose of this progression. The stories of the phallus that Del presents are basically stories that she mocks through irony and through a process of unmasking that parodies Mr. Chamberlain's self-exposure. Images of the phallus and stories about it recur several times in the chapter, and this in itself is an important irony: in the title chapter of this novel, in the story in which Del's mother makes her hopeful prediction about the lives of girls and women — a prediction often read literally as a straightforward affirmation of contemporary girls' and women's aspirations — the central antagonistic force that Del must contend with is a demonstration that seeks to affirm the status of women as passive observers of phallic power.

Images of the phallus all connect in one way or another with Art Chamberlain. First, Del and Naomi read about the phallus in the book they find — in another irony — in Naomi's mother's "old hope chest": "The male sexual organ in erection, we read, had been known to reach a length of fourteen inches" (122). Naomi then rolls out a length of chewing gum to represent the organ of " 'Mr. Chamberlain, the record breaker!' " (122). When she performs her trick with the chewing gum in front of Mr. Chamberlain, his remark (" 'That's quite a game you got there' ") seems to resonate more suggestively than Del's mother's remark (" 'Stop that, it's filthy' "), which, if it were not for Del's parenthetical explanation "(She meant the gum.)," would seem to be the more suggestive of these two responses. But by now we may tend to respond to Del's mother's remarks as if she were less capable of or interested in figurative speech and meaning, and to Mr. Chamberlain as if many of his remarks either mask their meanings or play with ambiguity. Mr. Chamberlain, after all, is the adult who incarnates ambiguity in this chapter, a character who is welcome in Del's mother's house, who has a sexual relationship with Fern Dogherty, and who is both the object of Del's fantasized desires and the subject who seems to accept the role that Del has cast for him.

The next image of the phallus presents it as part of a work of art in another medium, a sculpture. This is a representation at least twice removed from everyday life: first, it is Michelangelo's statue of David, and second, it is a photograph of that statue — and a photograph further qualified by its context in Del's mother's "art-and-architecture supplement to the encyclopedia" (126). When Del's mother shows the picture of David to Mr. Chamberlain, Del reflects: "A naked man. His marble thing hanging on him for everybody to look at; like a drooping lily petal" (126). But Mr. Chamberlain says he did not see the statue of David when he was in Italy, and deflects the conversation to his recollection of the real people he met there, and his alleged disappointment with the Italian father and daughter. It is Del's imagination that remains more literally preoccupied with the image, having less direct experience than Mr. Chamberlain with what the image might signify or represent.

The third image of the phallus is described through Del's account of Mr. Chamberlain masturbating in front of her. This episode shows, as powerfully as any passage in the novel, to what purposes and effects Del uses description, not only to define her experience, but also as a necessary protection, as a way not only of knowing the world, but of affirming her own subjectivity through writing. Her description becomes an effective countermeasure, or counterperformance to Mr. Chamberlain's. In "Baptizing," we will see another side of this purpose in Del's description of her relationship with Garnet French; but here, Del finds the language appropriate to respond to Mr. Chamberlain's performance, objectifying his phallus in a recognition, and a defense against, the ways in which Mr. Chamberlain seeks to objectify her through *his* performance.[18]

The episode takes place after Mr. Chamberlain has sent Del on a spying mission into Fern's bedroom, looking for incriminating letters. But all that Del has found are more texts about sexuality — doggerel rhymes (interestingly, the poem Del quotes is the only text in this chapter that presents a woman's point of view about sexual experience and describes it as in any way desirable for the woman [139]), or instructions about contraception; and, although Del recalls that words like "fuck" still "fired up lust at a great rate, like squirts of kerosene on bonfires," the simile itself captures just how brief and unsatisfactory this experience has become (139). Reading about sexuality will no longer replace more direct experience for Del; but the central irony is that her experience in this chapter will only reinforce the passive role in which almost all of her reading casts women, so that her only recourse, perhaps, will be to become a writer — one who can describe, and fend off, the role prescribed for her by describing, and in this way deflating, the power that Mr. Chamberlain thinks that he wields.

This experience represents Del's first major excursion from the imaginative conception of a sexual experience to the experience itself. As she recalls getting out of the car with Mr. Chamberlain, Del reflects on this transformational journey, remarking "Events were becoming real" (140). She continues to emphasize her separation from Mr. Chamberlain at this point, recalling that "He got out on his side, I got out on mine," and she also sharply distinguishes between the eroticism that has until this point fired her imagination and her body, and the effect of her anticipation of the actual event, in which she imagines herself passive, an object upon which something will be performed:

> Here in the half-shade above the creek I was cold, and so violently anxious to know what would be done to me that all the heat and dancing itch between my legs had gone dead, numb as if a piece of ice had been laid to it. (141)

Mr. Chamberlain's role is described from beginning to end as a performance, another kind of staging of an event. Even his initial exposure to Del is described in language that evokes the theatre and its distancing context, as well as the perverse catharsis of fear and surprise that the actor — Mr. Chamberlain — wishes to induce in his audience: "Mr. Chamberlain opened his jacket and loosened his belt, then unzipped himself. He reached in to part some inner curtains, and 'Boo!' he said" (141).

Del's description of Mr. Chamberlain's penis begins by immediately recalling the previous image of David's phallus and distinguishing Mr. Chamberlain's penis from it, and by reminding us that Del's only other context derives from what she has seen or read in pictures or texts: "Not at all like marble David's, it was sticking straight out in front of him, which I knew from my reading was what they did"

(141). To Del, it looks "blunt and stupid . . . vulnerable, playful and naïve, like some strong-snouted animal whose grotesque simple looks are some sort of guarantee of good will" (141). The description both subverts and converts the intentions of the actor, transforming them into the perceptions of the audience: here is a case in which the narrator's version of the story is sharply transformed by the reader's response to the narrator's intentions. Del recalls that the total effect is actually the "opposite of what beauty usually is," inviting us to speculate, perhaps, on how beauty manifests itself to Del (141). Presumably, beauty, unlike what Del sees before her eyes, is the opposite of raw (refined?), the opposite of ugly, the opposite of "playful, vulnerable, and naive," and, perhaps most importantly, the opposite of "some sort of guarantee of good will" (141). This definition might serve, not only to collapse Mr. Chamberlain's intentions, but to alert us to some of the touchstones of Munro's conceptions of *her* aesthetic intentions, or, more to the point, of Del's. What is made quite clear at the end of this description is the detachment that Del feels from the scene she is describing, and specifically from Mr. Chamberlain's penis: "It did not bring back any of my excitement, though. It did not seem to have anything to do with me" (141).

Only after she has demystified the phallus does Del turn to Mr. Chamberlain himself. Her description of his expression reinforces the staged aspect of this scene, but it also makes the first connections between the theatrical element of this performance and the "human" needs that the performance reveals. It is true to the nature of Del's experience, and revelatory of how her experience reflects the social norms she has described, that this first connection should be established as she watches Mr. Chamberlain:

> The face he thrust out at me, from his crouch, was blind and wobbling like a mask on a stick, and those sounds coming out of his mouth, involuntary, last-ditch human noises, were at the same time theatrical, unlikely. In fact the whole performance, surrounded by calm flowering branches, seemed imposed, fantastically and predictably exaggerated, like an Indian dance. (141)

Mr. Chamberlain's remark after he ejaculates and wipes his hands and Del's skirt — " 'Lucky for you? Eh?' " (142) — allows us another insight into his perceptions. It is, evidently, "lucky" for Del that he was only masturbating, that she was simply a witness at the event, because she has run no risk of getting pregnant; and it is also lucky for her that he has a handkerchief with which to wipe away any sign of the episode, so that there will be no possibility of *Del* being detected in any kind of transgression. And his final remark, the "only thing he said," confirms Del's role in his mind as a spectator, a witness, and his own role as orchestrator of the spectacle: " 'Quite a sight, eh?' " (142).

At this point in her narration, Del is becoming more aware of two related but divergent processes, which can be formulated as a paradox: the process of turning experiences into stories, either in anticipation or in retrospect, and the process through which her narration leads her to insights into her experience. Now she sees, however, that she cannot turn her experience with Mr. Chamberlain into a story, because she has lost her audience — Naomi having undergone a transformation during her illness — and because she cannot find a way to render Mr. Chamberlain in all his guises in the same story, just as she could not hang all of her pictures of Miss Farris together at the end of "Changes and Ceremonies." That is, she cannot find a way to turn it into a story within the novel we are reading — the first process described above. But of course we are reading the issue of the second process, which is the story about Mr. Chamberlain that makes up her narration, and that leads her to the insight she gains into what people take with them into their sexual lives. The passage in which Del describes both these processes is worth quoting in full, because it shows so clearly in what unexpected ways Mr. Chamberlain has helped her to perceive the transition from one set of poses and gestures to another, a transition that she can then generalize from to frame her understanding of both her fantasy and the reality of sexual experience. As well, this is the fullest depiction yet of one of the problems that Del will come up against so sharply in the "Epilogue," which is the persistence and endurance of reality, despite any of her attempts to treat it in or as fiction:

> So I had not the relief of making what Mr. Chamberlain had done into a funny, though horrifying, story. I did not know what to do with it. I could not get him back to his old role, I could not make him play the single-minded, simple-minded, vigorous, obliging lecher of my daydreams. My faith in simple depravity

had weakened. Perhaps nowhere but in daydreams did the trap door open so sweetly and easily, plunging bodies altogether free of thought, free of personality, into self-indulgence, mad bad license. Instead of that, Mr. Chamberlain had shown me, people take along a good deal — flesh that is not overcome but has to be thumped into ecstasy, all the stubborn puzzle and dark turns of themselves. (144–45)

The decision that Del comes to at the end of the chapter might seem simply to serve notice of her determination to resist her mother's prescriptions and the traditional female roles these prescriptions defy. But we cannot fail to notice the language that Del uses to parody the alternative male role, the decree that "men were supposed to be able to go out and take on all kinds of experiences and shuck off what they didn't want and come back proud" (147). Once this description has revealed the bravado and the hollowness of the male formula, it is difficult not to read Del's closing remark as both a record of her resolution and a wry confession of her naïveté as she looks back on this stage of her life: "Without even thinking about it, I had decided to do the same" (147). The admission restores some of the comedy and wistful humour that often accompanies Del's descriptions of her state of mind after one of her disillusionments. But the force of the insight provided by Mr. Chamberlain's version of sexual communication prevails; the "dark turns" that Del finds revealed so graphically in her recollection of his performance, she will soon discover, lie more subtly concealed, more ambiguously shaded, and closer to home than she might imagine.

"BAPTIZING": WORDLESS LOVE AND REAL LIFE

As the excerpt quoted earlier from her interview with Struthers makes clear, Munro did not compose the parts of *Lives of Girls and Women* in the order of its published form — the order in which we have been considering its chapters. She wrote "Baptizing," Munro explains to Struthers, after "Princess Ida," and after she had "picked out" "Age of Faith," "Changes and Ceremonies," and the title chapter from the novel she thought she was writing.[19] With its more extended form and in its position at what was once the end of the novel (before Munro added "Epilogue: The Photographer"), "Baptizing" works less as a self-contained story, and more richly as a chapter, than any other part of the book. It refers more often than any other chapter to what has come before — to the evolution of Del's relationships with her mother (and now, to her mother's surprising decline), with her father and Owen, with Naomi; to the wide arc of Del's whole development in a social and psychological world tightly circumscribed by Jubilee norms; to many of the stages of her progressive discoveries and disillusionments; and to several relationships that typify the directions Del might take to understand, escape, or imagine a Jubilee life.

By far the longest section in the book (at fifty-three pages, it is almost twice the length of "Heirs of the Living Body" and "Lives of Girls and Women"), "Baptizing" often brings the whole of *Lives of Girls and Women* to mind because it recapitulates many of the stories first told separately in the book's chapters, embedding and retelling them within a shorter time frame but a more extended form. Separated by spacing in the text into five coherent sections, "Baptizing" takes us through the evolution of three complementary, corrective versions of relationship for Del in her recollections of Clive, Jerry Storey, and Garnet French. "Baptizing" also implies another progressive relation between these stories, as Del will find it increasingly difficult to break free from her relationships with the three male figures or to redefine herself in the light of the insights she gains. In the final section of "Baptizing," it will be explicitly *un*clear to Del (and to her readers) what the relations might be between the worlds she names in her closing allusions to *"Garnet French"* and *"Real life"* (201).

The language and the style of the sections of "Baptizing" evolve in keeping with their treatments of the different relationships Del recalls. The opening section, with its depiction of Del's continuing separation from Naomi as the two girls follow different paths into adulthood, is narrated in a language and style that invite us to respond to much of this story as serious social comedy. The twinned perspectives of Del looking back on herself and of Del experiencing these episodes merge, as they do throughout *Lives of Girls and Women*, in Del's reliving of these episodes as she narrates them; but in the first section of "Baptizing," the voice of the older Del looking back often dominates the narration. This distance allows Del to describe but also to mock the whole constellation of clichés and codes of conduct that embody many of Jubilee's social norms and expectations, from the path to marriage that Naomi is taking through "Commercial" classes, the small intrigues of office life, and the Gay-la dance hall, to the psychological pap served up by the articles Del reads (and worries over) about men's and women's worldviews (150–51), to the sequence of rituals that she assembles into the story of her "date" with Clive (155–61).

The distance that Del achieves from these experiences through the wry tone of her recollections complements the detached perspectives she continues to hold of her identity and of her body. She can still imagine herself in melodramatic, theatrical contexts derived from the operas she listens to, and her description of the end of *Carmen* reveals how fascinated Del remains with the idea of an identity conceived, imagined, formulated as a kind of performance, an act, rather than an identity that is apparently natural, given, spontaneous, or pre-existent:

> Yet I loved most of all *Carmen*, at the end. . . . I was shaken, imagining the other surrender, more tempting, more gorgeous even than the surrender to sex — the hero's, the patriot's, Carmen's surrender to the final importance of gesture, image, self-created self. (153)

And if Del's imagination continues to conceive of a selfhood that is "self-created" as the most tempting surrender, her conception of her own body remains detached and largely a product of her reading; her body remains a text that she can only read in relation to other texts, rather than a more subjectively experienced, more fully integrated expression of her imaginative and sexual, social and biological being. The result is a kind of wry self-deprecation that nicely captures the tonal range of this first section: "I liked looking at the reproduction of Cézanne's 'Bathers' in the art supplement of the encyclopedia, then at myself naked in the glass. But the insides of my thighs quivered; cottage cheese in a transparent sack" (153). This perspective also creates the distance from which Del watches herself dancing with Clive at the Gay-la dance hall, or narrates her recollected evening with him, Naomi, and Bert Matthews. Del's language clearly signals her perceptions of her physical contact with Clive, or rather, of his contact with her, in her description of their kiss in Bert Matthews's car: "He bent over and pressed his face against mine and stuffed his tongue, which seemed enormous, wet, cold, crumpled, like a dishrag, into my mouth" (158). In its tone, its language, and its suggestion of her objectified role, the description recalls Del's recent experience with Mr. Chamberlain; and when Del recalls that Clive "rather roughly tickled [her] armored midriff," her language again suggests both the distance and the sharp-edged comedy that inform her perspective on her appearance in this section.

But as we have already learned, Naomi's rituals are not Del's, and there is little surprise in the way that this section traces the final separation between them. The stages of Del's description of being drunk, though, are interesting in their echoes of an earlier Munro story, "An Ounce of Cure," from her first book, *Dance of the Happy Shades*; and in the scene depicting Naomi's indignant confrontation with Del the following morning, it may be that Munro first discovered the powerfully ambiguous resonances of the question that would become the title of her 1978 book of linked stories:

> "Who do you think you are? Clive is not an idiot you know. He has a good job. He's an *insurance* adjustor. Who do you want to go out with? *High-school boys?*" (161)

In this book, in Naomi's voice, the question embodies the indignation that Jubilee reserves for any sign of ambition, any pretense at somehow being different, or better, recalling Aunt Elspeth's and Auntie Grace's perspectives in "Heirs of the Living Body." In *Who Do You Think You Are?*, the title and the stories explore the ironies of the question more fully, making its ambiguities more evident in the development of Rose's character. Here, the irony of the question, the play of levels of meaning that it conceals and reveals, is imperceptible to Naomi. But to a narrator and reader like Del, with her consistent awareness of the sound, the sense, and the texture of words, Naomi's rebuke might signify more than Naomi intends.

Del's recollection in the next section of her relationship with Jerry Storey is a variation and development of the story in the first part of "Baptizing." One route into adulthood — towards the "normal life" best exemplified in Naomi's story (161) — has been abandoned as impossible for Del. But this second story is less easily given up, because in some ways it more closely reflects Del's own ambitions; and following it to its possibly happy ending might also allow Del to avoid an open break with her mother, because the story of academic success for Del, of scholarships and a university career, is one that her mother has been nourishing for a long time. In her recollections of her relationship with Jerry Storey, Del traces the attractions, the frustrations, and finally the sterility of a total rejection of Jubilee norms. Jerry Storey's pursuit of a life beyond Jubilee depends on his nearly total devotion to a monkish life of the mind; and one of the prices he must pay for this stance is a curious intolerance for language that does not refer directly, purposefully, systematically to the world at large. More generally, Jerry distrusts works of the imagination, including literary works, and this attitude defines one of the impasses between him and Del. Another way of putting it is to suggest that Jerry Storey distrusts, or cannot understand figurative language — language that at once evokes something beyond itself and calls attention to itself, to its syntax and style, like the passage from *Look Homeward, Angel* that he reads with such exasperation (167). The same stance, perhaps, is evident in his approach to the mystery of another kind of figure — to Del's body.

Del's perception of Jerry's stance allows us to draw a valuable distinction between the ways that she and Jerry conceive of themselves, and this is one of the differences that Del has been alluding to in different contexts throughout *Lives of Girls and Women*. In "Changes and Ceremonies," we recall Del's description of Frank Wales, after he has taken the role of the Pied Piper and Del has fallen in love with him: he walks like "someone who does not need either to efface or call attention to himself," and his very clothes seem to be signs of the ordinariness that, for Del, also conceals a mystery: "Every day he wore a blue-gray sweater, darned at the elbow, and this smoky color, so ordinary, reticent, and mysterious, seemed to me his color, the color of his self" (110). Del's conceptions of her own identity are rarely so natural or ordinary. More often, her descriptions invite us to consider the ambiguities she perceives, not only between appearance and reality, but also among the various versions of selfhood that she inhabits, creates, and presents. In the first section of "Baptizing," we recall, she refers to her fascination with the "self-created self" at the end of *Carmen*. In the contrast that she now draws between Jerry Storey's and her own visions and versions of selfhood, we can see the clearest illustration of Del's own "self-created" self and its more fluid and changeable shape. Del recalls that although when she was younger she laughed at Jerry, her attitude has changed:

> ... I thought now that there was something admirable, an odd, harsh grace about the way he conformed to type, accepting his role in Jubilee, his necessary and gratifying absurdity, with a fatalism, even gallantry, which I would never have been able to muster myself.... He could not do otherwise; he was what he seemed. I, whose natural boundaries were so much more ambiguous, who soaked up protective coloration wherever it might be found, began to see that it might be restful to be like Jerry. (165–66)

The impossible element in Jerry's stance, as in Frank Wales's, is that both appear to be what they are; both are what they seem. For Del, the relations between appearance and reality are more charged, more mysterious, more ambiguous, and one of the areas in which this ambiguity is most sharply revealed to her is in conceptions, perceptions, and presentations of self. Jerry has found a way of "conforming to type," of accepting his singularity in Jubilee, that Del will not be able to create without recreating Jubilee itself; her own relation with Jubilee is far less resigned, far more double-edged, many-edged than Jerry's. Jubilee is at once the social, natural, and psychological environment that has so narrowly defined her possibilities; the flat, ordinary world before her eyes that might, like Uncle Benny's version of the Wawanash river, conceal mysterious depths; and the setting for the banal, removed, but also threatening, possibly dangerous world of boys and men that lies alongside her own. And Del's conception of herself — of what we might begin to see, as she does herself, as her "self-created self" — complements, reflects, and responds to her visions of Jubilee, a territory that enthralls her, in both senses of the word, in ways foreign to Jerry and his worldview.

The comedy of Jerry's (allegedly) scientifically motivated inspection of Del's body is the last of the series of stories leading up to Del's relationship with Garnet French. Although it is comic both in Del's recollection and her experience, it is also the next to last version of

Del's passivity in these stories, as well as the last story in which Del will imagine the body (here, hers and Jerry's) as foreign territory. But the comedy of the situation and its outcome cannot wholly distract us from Del's perceptions of Jerry's possible intentions, or from the ways in which the cartoon-strip language that they use continues on another level the pattern of performance, of the safer distances in theatrical stagings of events, that has typified Del's sexual life to this point. The only difference is that here the performance, the stage, the theatre are less formalized, less social, and closer to the less predictable rituals of real life. But the comedy cannot entirely mask the scene's place in relation to Del's earlier experiences:

> He stood by the bed looking down at me, making faint comical noises of astonishment. Did he feel my body as inappropriate, as unrealizable, as I did his? Did he want to turn me into some comfortable girl with lust uncomplicated by self-consciousness, a girl without sharp answers, or a large vocabulary, or any interest in the idea of order in the universe, ready to cuddle him down? We both giggled. (169)

The bathos of this episode resolves Jerry's and Del's discomfort with any physical expression of relationship by barring any further experimentation. But it also prepares us for Del's separation from Jerry and the path he is following out of Jubilee. Because of this chapter's title and the framework that defines Del's relationship with Garnet French, the chaste and religious devotion with which she and Jerry study for their scholarship examinations (172–73) seems in retrospect to become a pale and ironic reflection of Del's and Garnet's devotions. And Del's closing observation in this section—"My need for love had gone underground, like a canny toothache" (173) — reaffirms the connections among these three stories of relationship, each of them exploring Del's alternatives in trying to satisfy her need — alternatives which are successively, if increasingly painfully discarded.

Del's story of her relationship with Garnet French is, of course, the novel's most sustained exploration of Del's sexual initiation, and it reveals to us most fully how the life of her body comes into being and informs her imaginative development. But Del never allows us to lose sight of the ways in which this story is also embedded in its setting in Jubilee, within Del's unfolding depiction of the boys and men who inhabit her world, and most importantly, within the world of words that has so consistently figured in the ordering of Del's recreation of her past.

The framework of the story, like the title of the chapter, suggests an irony that develops to its most powerful expression in Garnet's attempted baptizing of Del in the river. Del first sees Garnet at a revival meeting (in the Town Hall, also the site of the school operettas) in which the audience is exhorted to repent of their sins and be saved; and Garnet is there is because he has been saved from a life of violence by a Baptist minister who had converted him in jail. The salvation that Del will find for a time with Garnet, though, has little to do with religious conviction, and less to do with the delights, puzzlements, and inspiration that she finds in language. It is firmly, wordlessly grounded in physical apprehension, sensation, and intuition, and we are made aware of these dimensions, of their inexplicable mystery and of their development, from the opening scene onwards.

When Del first sees Garnet across the hall, she suddenly thinks that he will come over to stand beside her, but quickly recognizes and dismisses this thought as "nonsense; like a recognition in an opera, or some bad, sentimental, deeply stirring song" (175). But uncannily, in a confirmation of the inexplicable but powerful current of physical attraction between Del and Garnet, reality is about to confirm Del's seemingly melodramatic daydreaming; we have come full circle from her fantasy of love for Frank Wales and its real theatrical setting in *The Pied Piper*.

The reality of physical attraction can only be understood or confirmed for Del through physical sensation — in this case, through touch, and Del renders their first physical contact in a description that vividly evokes the stages of intimacy proposed, attempted, and fulfilled by the approach of their hands on the back of the chair in the town hall (177). Here is another route that might connect the surface of the everyday world with its impossibly separate depths — a relation and connection confirmed when Del describes her reaction three days later as she meets Garnet on the street while she is walking with Jerry Storey after school: she recalls that she was "Dizzy at this expected, yet unhoped-for reappearance, solid intrusion of the legendary into the real world." (178).

In the realm she enters with Garnet, Del's previous conceptions of the body, her own as well as others', dissolves as she learns a new language that, unlike the one that we read in the previous two sections of "Baptizing," conveys Del's immediate, intuitive apprehension of this experience. There is less of a distancing effect in this section, very little irony, very little of the detachment that produces some of the comic effects that we saw in the previous sections. Instead, Del's language opens out moments of quiet exaltation, of a silent wondering and marveling that we have only read at a few points in the novel before this section. Just as Del spoke of the "surrender" at the end of *Carmen* to a "self-created self," she now speaks of surrender in a different context, thinking about her early "approaches to sex" with Garnet in his truck: "Sex seemed to me all surrender — not the woman's to the man but the person's to the body, an act of pure faith, freedom in humility" (181). This conception has replaced the gender-bound surrender implied, if not demanded, by Mr. Chamberlain's performance and by some of the texts Del has read; this is a surrender of self-consciousness, and it crosses sexual and gendered boundaries. Furthermore, it implies a "pure faith" that Del looked for earlier in the church and in God, and that in this chapter is connected with baptismal rites.

But this surrender to the body is bound up with another kind of surrender, one that we might see as eventually bearing less desirable implications for Del: the surrender of words and all that they signify in Del's imaginative life. Del makes it clear in several ways throughout this section that her relationship with Garnet depends on them not talking about it; their apprehension of each other occurs at a different level:

> Nothing that could be said by us would bring us together; words were our enemies. What we knew about each other was only going to be confused by them. This was the knowledge that is spoken of as "only sex," or "physical attraction." I was surprised, when I thought about it — am surprised still — at the light, even disparaging tone that is taken, as if this was something that could be found easily, every day. (183)

With Garnet, Del is exposed to a world almost diametrically opposed to the one she inhabited with Jerry Storey. Paradoxically, Jerry's reality is both complex and flat for Del; she describes it as "dense and complicated but appallingly unsecretive" (184). Del describes the mysterious and wordless reality she inhabits with Garnet, in contrast, as "something not far from what I thought animals must see, the world without names" (184). This is a pre-verbal world, a world of the instincts; but in order to live in it fully with Garnet, Del would have to submit to other rituals of purification as well.

The warmest, most detailed description in this novel of a house and of a family's life within their house is contained in Del's recollection of her visit with Garnet's family for Sunday dinner. Here, out in the countryside beyond Jubilee, Del finds an extended family that lives its own more elaborated version of the life that Garnet has shown her. Relationship, sexuality, natural and seasonal cycles, idiosyncrasy, eccentricity, and the accommodating social structures of this family all interpenetrate easily and visibly: two boys fight playfully, savagely, and silently in the yard; Garnet's sisters take Del to show her the creek (which once flooded the house) and the newborn kittens in the barn; Garnet shows her his list of girls' names carved with a knife on the porch (each with an "x" added to signify Garnet's " 'Military secret!' " [187]) and then adds hers and kisses her in front of the family; and the meal that they all eat, in contrast to the meals that always dissatisfy Del in her mother's house, is a vividly chaotic, nourishing, richly satisfying occasion. And Del's acknowledgement of her pleasure in this setting — "There is no denying I was happy in that house" (188) — affirms that this is an admission that surprises her.

The return from this dinner is also the occasion for Del's and Garnet's first lovemaking; Del's description of this episode has attracted much critical attention.[20] The opening reminds us of Del's typical recourse to images of theatre and performance: "I had always thought that our eventual union would have some sort of special pause before it, a ceremonial beginning, like a curtain going up on the last act of a play" (188). But reality is less orchestrated, and Garnet too impatient, so that Del finds herself not only entangled in her own clothes, but trying to hold his pants up so that "the white gleam of his buttocks" will not reveal them to passersby (188).

Their fall into the peonies bordering Del's house accentuates the apparently improbable, but also fitting setting for their first sexual encounter. This is not simply Del's "defloration," but a crucial break in the social order that defines the relationship between mother and daughter, under the mother's roof. When she sees the blood on her leg, Del recalls that "the glory of the whole episode" became clear to her (189); we might recall that early in "Lives of Girls and Women," Del explains that it was "glory [she] was after" on the streets of Jubilee (119). Del "had to mention it to somebody," and so she tells her mother a story about a cat, a "big striped tom" "tearing a bird apart" (189); the plot, imagery, and characters Del chooses to compose this short but striking story provide us with insight into the ways she would like to present this incident, and to whom. Of course her mother misses Del's cues, which are necessarily figurative; Del cannot openly announce to her mother that she is not a virgin and that she made love for the first time with Garnet French the night before at the side of the house, and that they fell into the peonies. But perhaps she would like her mother to know, and like her mother to see the evidence of her successful consummation of this rite of passage. And yet Del's story, with its explicit suggestion of violence and death, transforms the experience into an unmotivated assault, and also into a natural occurrence in the animal world, so that Del creates a distance and a setting that disguise, reveal, and define the experience in terms that her mother cannot apprehend as fully as Del's readers.

The full blossoming of Del's sexual relationship with Garnet complements the withering of her hopes for a scholarship. But as she enters more completely into the "world without names" that she inhabits with Garnet, we can see Del becoming aware of facets of Garnet's nature and of her own that anticipate their separation. Del is spending her first summer in town; her mother has decided that the men are happier alone in the house on the Flats Road. When Del visits this male enclave, she finds that her role has become more closely defined, and that she is not allowed to drink beer like her younger brother. Uncle Benny's remark, " 'No good ever come of any girl that drunk beer,' " is exactly what Del "had heard Garnet say, the same words" (191). All three of the males — her father, Uncle Benny, and Owen — treat Del with a new sense of distance and difference, as if she now inhabits a separate reality; one result of this new delineation, perhaps, is the sense of strangeness, of detachment and alienation, with which Del observes herself and her surroundings as she walks back into town (191–92).

The other separation Del begins to feel lies closer to home, and is more central to her development as a writer. In a passage that anticipates Del's doubled role as an observer of and participant in her own life at the end of this chapter, she recalls how she begins to address herself in the third person: "I talked to myself about myself, saying *she. She is in love. She has just come in from being with her lover. Seed runs down her legs*" (192). This doubled perspective, we will see, begins to operate in several other realms of experience as well, including Del's treatments of reality in her fiction.

The fifth and final section of "Baptizing" depicts the scene in the Wawanash River between Garnet and Del. The river that runs through Jubilee has run throughout *Lives of Girls and Women*: in "The Flats Road" as a source of literal and imaginative sustenance in Uncle Benny's world; in "Heirs of the Living Body" as the setting for Del's walk with Mary Agnes Oliphant when they come upon the dead cow; in "Changes and Ceremonies" and "Epilogue: The Photographer" as Miss Farris's and Marion Sherriff's means of suicide. In its place as an ironic baptismal font in this section, as the late summer setting for Garnet's attempt to immerse Del in his version of a Jubilee life, the river acquires further significance, and the whole natural landscape of the novel enters into a more deeply ambiguous relationship with the landscape of Del's own consciousness. To immerse herself in the Wawanash, to yield to Garnet's wish, might seem to be like yielding fully to a life of the senses, or yielding fully to the body; but there are too many signs in this novel that the river is a more ambiguous vessel, a natural element that can both nourish and kill.

Garnet's role in this deadly serious play in the river is made quite clear to us, and we can see how Del's successful struggle to resist being "baptized" returns her to the world she formerly inhabited. But what may not immediately be as clear is Del's own complicity in Garnet's assumptions, her own responsibility for creating the relationship in which Garnet leads and is led to this moment. Recalling their struggle in the water, Del comes to several realizations that complicate our reading of this scene so that we cannot simply, or unilaterally condemn Garnet for trying to subjugate her. Del recalls her surprise that Garnet, or anybody, should have thought he had "real power" over her:

> I was too amazed to be angry, I forgot to be frightened, it seemed to me impossible that he should not understand that all the

powers I granted him were in play, that he himself was — in play, that I meant to keep him sewed up in his golden lover's skin forever, even if five minutes before I had talked about marrying him. This was clear as day to me, and I opened my mouth to say whatever would make it clear to him, and I saw that he knew it all already; this was what he knew, that I had somehow get his good offerings with my deceitful offerings, whether I knew it or not, matching my complexity and play-acting to his true intent. (197–98)

The insights Del gains here show her own "dark turns," including a capacity for "play-acting" that objectifies Garnet, preserving him in the role she has assigned him for the duration of this game, the role of a "golden lover." It is not only Del who is practised on, and not only boys and men who practise on girls and women; Del sees that she has countered the power of Garnet's "true intent" with her own less transparent strategies. But she also realizes — and this is an insight that Del gains in various forms throughout the novel, an insight that drives her towards autonomy and isolation, towards independence and towards an increasing preoccupation with her past — that this is, essentially, what defines her life, this "complexity and play-acting," and that she finally cannot surrender her "self-created self" because it is both what she is and what she creates. As we have seen throughout the novel, Del is a narrator who recalls her past and recreates herself, who both remembers her youth and continually enacts and re-enacts the development of her imagination. She remembers herself as she writes fiction; she recalls the past as she recreates Jubilee. Now, separating from Garnet, she is about to re-enter the world that she composes throughout *Lives of Girls and Women*, the world *with* names, and the world of words.

Del's recollections of this crucial break with Garnet *are* a kind of baptism, but not the baptism Garnet desires: she is baptized into distance, and the first sign we see of this stance is her doubled perspective on herself in the closing section of this chapter. In order to become a writer, Del needs to preserve and develop the detachment that has been inscribed in her life by Jubilee norms, but that has also been fostered by her own developing consciousness, by her own talent to draw on this detachment in order to observe, describe, and understand her life. Garnet teaches Del about the immersion in the body that she has desired for so long, but Del also needs her own life, and at the end of "Baptizing" we find her balanced precariously between the two latest versions of the polarities she has been dissolving, accommodating, or resolving throughout this novel.

Del's return to the world is an entrance into familiar territory, as she makes clear on her walk from the river back into Jubilee (199). But her own consciousness has been fragmented, and the worlds that present themselves to her do not lie as easily "alongside" each other as Uncle Benny's and her family's do in "The Flats Road." In fact, the only way in which Del will be able to accommodate these worlds will be to write them down, to evoke them in fiction; and we can see how the pull of both of these realities — of *"Garnet French"* and of *"Real life"* — has reproduced itself in her own consciousness, so that she both suffers and observes herself suffering. Del remembers looking at herself in the mirror:

> Without diminishment of pain I observed myself; I was amazed to think that the person suffering was me, for it was not me at all; I was watching. I was watching, I was suffering. I said into the mirror a line from Tennyson, from my mother's *Complete Tennyson* that was a present from her old teacher, Miss Rush. I said it with absolute sincerity, absolute irony. *He cometh not, she said.* (200)

This accommodation of two complementary perspectives, of this doubled vision of the watcher and the participant, the witness of her own suffering and the sufferer herself, is an internalized version of the accommodations Del must make throughout the novel. It requires an imagination that can describe and enact its own consciousness as fully, as subjectively and objectively, and in as much detail as if it were the "real life" that Del believes she will now move into. But the closing sentences of "Baptizing" show how, even as Del emerges from Garnet's reality into the world she knew before, the world without love, her imagination continues to create alternate versions of "real life," even in the process of affirming that she has put her daydreams behind her:

> Now at last without fantasies or self-deception, cut off from the mistakes and confusion of the past, grave and simple, carrying a

small suitcase, getting on a bus, like girls in movies leaving home,
convents, lovers, I supposed I would get started on my real life.
Garnet French, Garnet French, Garnet French.
Real life. (201)

Del cannot render her state of mind without transforming it, without commenting on the implications of the insight she believed she had gained. Following the progress of the opening sentence above, we might notice it turning inwards towards its own creation to comment on the image of Del seemingly free, finally, of her fantasies and self deception: this image, which we might want to read as Del's straightforward assessment of her state of mind, becomes more problematic when Del introduces the comparison "like girls in movies" — a turn of phrase that summons up all the worlds of theatre, of performance, melodrama, of stories themselves that we have watched Del read and refer to so often. The girls in the movies, presumably, are acting out roles similar to the one Del watches herself acting in her "real life"; but Del's closing reflection that she "supposed" she would get started on her real life might only sharpen our perception that the supposition might be flawed — that the only satisfactory way for Del to get started on her real life will be to write about it. And the closing, repeated invocation of Garnet's name leaves us with a simulacrum of Del's sombre affirmation that there are at least two more worlds, a wordless world without names in love, and a world that she names beyond love. But where in Del's imagination Garnet French and real life can separate, meet, or lie alongside each other is a question that only fiction could propose.

"EPILOGUE: THE PHOTOGRAPHER": HOW DEL WRITES

The last and the shortest section of *Lives of Girls and Women* was the one that gave Munro the most trouble — to the point that she changed her mind several times about including it at all. As Thomas Tausky has shown in detail in an article published in 1986, " 'What Happened to Marion?': Art and Reality in *Lives of Girls and Women*," the Munro papers collected at the University of Calgary, which include several earlier drafts of this section, provide a fascinating glimpse of Munro's difficulties and of her process of revision.[21]

The epilogue is also the part of the novel that has given readers the most difficulty. Some have found it an unconvincing or unnecessary justification of Del's, and perhaps of Munro's purposes and techniques in writing fiction, while others have found it successful on both these counts; some have found it too autobiographical, too much in Munro's voice rather than Del's.[22] But the difficulties with this section, whether they are Munro's or her readers', need not obscure how this "Epilogue" is intended to function in relation to the whole book.

Throughout the novel, we have seen Del reflecting on the sound and sense of individual words; on her various forms of reading, and on various kinds of writing; and on the stories that she hears, that others tell, that she herself shapes and tells. In this final section, Del tries to define, not only what she writes, or why she writes, although she explores both of these areas, but also *how* she writes. That she fails to explain this fully is an eloquent illustration of Del's apprehension of fiction's ultimately mysterious nature. Although Del is left dissatisfied with her (unwritten) novel about Caroline and the photographer — and then further frustrated with the heartbreaking impossibility of writing fiction that will "really" render a setting, a character, an experience, or a life — we may be left more content with Del's necessarily inadequate explanation of her fictional techniques and purposes. Like the earlier themes Del explores, writing itself will finally be revealed as an unknowable mystery, and this will be the final illuminating correction to her vision in this book. It is an insight that allows Del to close her narration and begin her novel — because this section also begins to transform *Lives of Girls and Women*, the novel we have been reading, into the novel that Del is about to write — with an affirmation that is an awareness of any writer's limitations, an acknowledgement of mystery, and above all a declaration of independence and inheritance.

The first major question that Del explores in this closing section raises an issue that has troubled her throughout the book, and that sooner or later engages most writers and readers: what is "real" in fiction? Munro's original title for *Lives of Girls and Women*, we recall, was "Real Life," and we have seen how often, and in how many different guises, the question of what is real has arisen throughout the book. Now, however, the question centres on the powers and the nature of fiction itself, and on how a writer conceives of her art.

a long crack running down it, somewhat diagonally, starting a bit before the middle and ending up at the bottom corner, next to the Chainway Store.

What happened to Bobby Sherriff when he had to go into the ~~the~~ Asylum? What happened Marion to ~~Madame~~? Not to Caroline. What happened to Marion?

These are questions which persist, in spite of novels. It is ~~strange~~ a shock, when you have dealt so cunningly, ~~comprehensively~~ powerfully with reality, to come back and find it still there, diffuse, mysterious, dull, broken, simple, amazing. I did not suddenly realise, looking at the Herald-Advance wall, and Bobby Sherriff's unrevealing face, that I had lost my novel. I knew already I had lost it, and I h never did face that fact directly; I just stopped going to look at it, finally stopped thinking about it altogether, though occasionally I would be reminded by unlikely things - a board fence, a dog in the street, a phrase in conversation - and I would feel a quick ache, an almost formal compunction for having let it all die, because I ~~can having~~ ~~though daring~~ locked the ~~power, strength,~~ everything that was needed to bring it to birth. Nothing immediately took its place. I did not foresee that one day I would be concerned with that porch where we were sitting, the yellow stucco wall of the house, Bobby Sherriff's mother's ~~beds~~ also beds of geometric flower-beds edged with white, would delphiniums and zinnias. Also with the houses on either side, (futiles, I would want to re-create with mad heartbreaking accuracy) chamomiles the street, I would want to make lists of the streets, and of the stores and businesses along the main street, and of people's names, family names, and of the tombstones in the cemetery, the verses written on them, the names on the cenotaph, the titles of all the movies that played at the Lyceum theatre from 1940, say, to 1950. Such lists would be a comfort, ~~though~~ though they would not ~~implement~~ contain what I wanted, ~~Everybody knows phrases like these~~ in the end I would have to see that they could not contain what I wanted, because what I wanted was everything - every ~~stroke of light on dark and walls~~ layer of speech and thought, every grief, ~~clunk of cowbells,~~ every smell, ~~hand~~, pot-hole, pain, crack, delusion, ~~every bug or wrapped loaf~~, held still and held together, radiant, everlasting. What tricks can manage that?

"Believe me," said Bobby Sherriff wistfully, relieving me of my fork, napkin, and empty plate, "I wish you luck in your life." I took them as natural offerings, then, people's wishes, ~~It seemed a natural thing for everybody to be wishing me.~~

"Yes," I said, instead of thank-you.

Revised typescript of the conclusion of "Epilogue."
Special Collections, University of Calgary Libraries.

And because of Del's role in this section as an interpreter, a commentator on her own fiction, the question brings home to us its inevitable corollary: how do readers conceive of their art, of the fictions that they shape from the text?

The novel that Del carries in her head originates in two questions that she poses, questions that she will discover cannot be answered satisfactorily in fiction. One is the question she poses to herself while talking to Bobby Sherriff on the porch of the Sherriff house: *"What Happened to Marion?"* (209). The other is the question implied by Del's contemplation of Marion Sherriff's picture in the hall of the high school, and explored through Del's creation of the character of the photographer in her unwritten novel: what kind of representation of reality is a photograph, and how should we read photographs?

Neither the explanation provided by Fern Dogherty for Marion's suicide nor Del's mother's reasoned objection to Fern's analysis is enough for Del: she needs to write a novel which will comprise a different kind of "explanation," one that takes as its points of departure the photograph of Marion and the inexplicable fact of her suicide. But the photograph — a seemingly documentary representation of Marion's appearance — and the suicide — an act which would seem to demand an explanation derived from the circumstances in Marion's life that might have led up to her death — do not inspire Del to write a novel that operates as *Lives of Girls and Women* seems to be doing. *Lives of Girls and Women* seems to be a piece of fine realist fiction, a novel that shows us a faithful, detailed representation of real life, of more or less plausible characters acting in plausible ways in recognizable settings. But Del's novel departs from these conventions. Caroline, the character that Del creates, does not represent Marion physically in the least:

> ... *Caroline!* Her name was Caroline. She came ready-made into my mind, taunting and secretive, blotting out altogether that pudgy Marion, the tennis player. Was she a witch? Was she a nymphomaniac? Nothing so simple! (204)

Del's creation, "wayward and light as a leaf," is an enchantress who acts in ways unthinkable, inconceivable in the Jubilee we have come to know through Del's narration (204). She is a seductress, one who picks the most unlikely partners and who seems to act sexually rather than being acted upon sexually; but she is also, in ways somewhat reminiscent of Del's experiences in the title chapter and in "Baptizing," described as a passive agent:

> She was a sacrifice, spread for sex on moldy uncomfortable tombstones, pushed against the cruel bark of trees, her frail body squashed into the mud and hen dirt of barnyards, supporting the killing weight of men, but it was she, more than they, who survived. (204–05)

We might see elements of Del's experience as a girl growing up in Jubilee transformed in her creation of Caroline, so that the character not only "blots out" Marion, but affords Del herself a more richly ambiguous sexual life, one that allows her, and not the men with their "killing weight," to endure. Regardless of what elements of Del's experience we might read into her creation of Caroline, though, we can see that Caroline and Marion are worlds and conventions apart. Marion (and her photograph) is a part of the Jubilee world that Del has recollected throughout *Lives of Girls and Women*, whereas Caroline belongs in a world that Del has created for her own fictional purposes, a world less mimetically reflective of Jubilee. The fictional world of Del's novel, she recalls, was "true" rather than "real," and it revealed all of the depths and mysteries that she had always perceived to lie beneath everyday reality; and yet her description of this fictional universe opens with the same reference to mental imagery that evoked Del's confusion over Miss Farris's different poses and gestures, and that now forcefully returns us to one dimension of a photographer's art:

> All pictures. The reasons for things happening I seemed vaguely to know, but could not explain; I expected all that would come clear later. The main thing was that it seemed true to me, not real but true, as if I had discovered, not made up, such people and such a story, as if that town was lying close behind the one I walked through every day. (206)

Del's description is not a realist's credo. The "truth" of her conception has little to do with realism's aims; the novel is "true" in that it presents what she imagines, what she sees in her "pictures" of

Caroline, the Halloways, the Jubilee she has transformed for her own purposes. None of this is "real" in the same way that Del's evocations of her own Jubilee life have been, and will be in the novel Del will write and we have just read. The Halloway novel gives Del a coherent world, true to its own nature, true to her own intentions, but not "true" to the less predictable real world that her novel transforms in ways that are more apparent to us, and to Del, than the transformations necessarily produced in *any* work of fiction, including *Lives of Girls and Women*. The Halloway fiction is not necessarily worse fiction, or weaker fiction; it is only fiction that more visibly departs from the conventions of realism. In its way, it is just as "true" as *Lives of Girls and Women*.

It is tempting to read the role of the photographer in the Halloway novel as an important comment on the stance and function of the writer, particularly the writer of realist fiction. A more plausible photographer, taking photographs like the one of Marion that hangs in the main hall of the school, would practice an art more in keeping with our suppositions about realist fiction. His photographs would not transform their subjects to expose horrifying revelations. Real photographs, as Del is discovering about the photograph of Marion (and as we might discover, along with Del, about realist fiction), announce a paradox. On one hand, they seem to represent reality in images that read like documentary, literal transcriptions, so that when we see a face in a photograph, we are apt to say, that *is* the person it represents. In other words, we do not usually read photographs with much attention to their artifice, to their *re*presentation of reality. But on the other hand, a photograph, by virtue of its seemingly perfect rendition of a part of reality — a face, for example — becomes impenetrable, impossible to interpret, because it seems to offer no gap between that which it represents — the original face — and the representation — the photograph. Realism, Del is in the process of discovering — and we have been discovering throughout this novel — performs a similar illusion. But her photographer only seems to wield the realist's instruments of perception; like Del's Caroline, he departs radically from convention, so that his photographs, like the "pictures" from which Del constructs her Halloway novel, reveal "truths" rather than "real" images. Of all Jubilee, only Caroline is not afraid of him; one way of understanding her impassioned pursuit of the photographer is to read it as her (and Del's) desperate search for the "truth" of her own nature, which this photographer (in a neat reversal of the failure of the Jubilee photographer who took Marion's picture to reveal in it any truth about Marion to Del) might be able to reveal. At this point Del's novel ends by returning to its point of departure, the mystery of Marion's suicide, the enigma of her photograph, just as *Lives of Girls and Women* will soon end by returning to its point of departure. The photographer vanishes, and Caroline, like Marion, walks into the Wawanash River (205). Del's account of her first attempt at a novel may be completed, but the reality that she drew on for its creation remains to push Del into another inadequate attempt to recreate her past. When Del accepts Bobby Sherriff's invitation to have a piece of cake and some lemonade, she realizes, sitting on the Sherriff porch, that reality, in all of its ordinary, everyday, flat impenetrability, has persisted, in spite of her novel about it. Not only that: it is her novel, and not reality itself, that has lost power, she realizes (208). The writer's art, regardless of its conventions, creates a reality which, regardless of its own "truth," is both autonomous *and* related to the world it refers to, however diffuse or symbolic this connection may be. Paradoxically, it is in the Halloway novel that we (along with Del) may be able to see more clearly the relations between real world and fictional world. In *Lives of Girls and Women* itself, the relations are more mysterious, for all of realism's supposed mimetic properties; and Del is discovering this mystery at the heart of what will be her art as she sits with Bobby Sherriff, who is himself only the last of the several Jubilee eccentrics who have confronted Del with unknowable and yet alluring realities.

While Bobby Sherriff explains to Del (in another variation on the title of Munro's 1978 book of stories) that he knows who she is (" 'I know you .... Didn't you think I knew who you were?' " [208]), Del is confronted with the realization that whatever else it might do, fiction does not provide explanations of reality. This realization reaffirms the insights Del has been gaining about inexplicable but enduring realities throughout her story; as well, it helps her to see how she might write a novel like *Lives of Girls and Women*, and helps us to understand how we might read it:

> And what happened, I asked myself, to Marion? Not to Caroline. *What happened to Marion?* .... Such questions persist, in

spite of novels. It is a shock, when you have dealt so cunningly, powerfully, with reality, to come back and find it still there. (209)

Reality is, indeed, "still there," and as Del muses on its pervasive, persistent, insistent presence, she returns for the last time to one origin of her novel about Caroline and the photographer — the photograph of Marion — and is led from there to her famous insight, which resolves for one luminous moment Del's lifelong experience of surface and depth, appearance and reality, flat ordinary details and the mysteries they proclaim, into an image announcing the presence and plurality of *all* these qualities:

> His [Bobby's] sister's photographed face hung in the hall of the high school, close to the persistent hiss of the drinking fountain. Her face was stubborn, unrevealing, lowered so that shadows had settled in her eyes. People's lives, in Jubilee as elsewhere, were dull, simple, amazing and unfathomable — deep caves paved over with kitchen linoleum. (210)

It is important to notice, as Del does, that it is Marion's *photographed* face that hangs in the hall — that it is this *image* of her face that is "stubborn, unrevealing." From this perception of what the photographer's art does *not* render, Del is able to reach her insight about people's lives everywhere, in and beyond Jubilee. The passage ends where *Lives of Girls and Women* begins: not with the mystery concealed by surfaces, but with the surface itself. It is the ordinary "kitchen linoleum" underfoot, usually faded, that covers the "deep caves." The passive agency suggested by the structure of the closing phrase — "Paved [over] with" by someone, no-one, or everyone — appears to offer us an indication of unconscious, ritualized, or unintentional behaviour; but the more explicit suggestion of intentionality and domesticating, civilizing concealment conveyed by "paved" offers us a fitting complementary reading, so that the syntax and vocabulary of the phrase enact at one more level the vision of complementary worlds, complementary visions that Del has been creating.

From recording this insight Del moves to the first of the novel's two conclusions, narrated from the vantage point of the adult Del, recalling that she did not realize, sitting on the porch with Bobby

Sherriff, that she would "one day ... be so greedy for Jubilee" (210). In "Heirs of the Living Body," Del gains an important insight into the kind of mistake her Uncle Craig is making writing his history of Wawanash County; now, she extends the compass of that insight to include her own "misguided" impulse to "write things down" (210). This is an interesting formulation, suggesting that making fiction might depend on lists, on "accuracy," on reporting, like Uncle Craig did, what took place, why, to whom, when, and where. But Del's process of correction and adjustment continues: "writing things down" will not give her what she wants, she realizes, any more than Uncle Craig's history did. It is her realization of what she really wants, of what fiction might really be capable of giving her, that will return Del in memory to her moment with Bobby Sherriff on the porch.

Del wants detail — the grainy particulars, all of the elements that all of her senses can apprehend — in order to read them into language and shape them through her imagination to give them the fictional form that will bring her past alive. This is the kind of "list" that Del realizes she needs, and this is what she "writes down" as her last insight:

> And no list could hold what I wanted, for what I wanted was every last thing, every layer of speech and thought, stroke of light on bark or walls, every smell, pothole, pain, crack, delusion, held still and held together — radiant, everlasting. (210)

With this passage we have reached the point closest in time to the present of Del the writer, looking back over her past and over the way she looks at her past, learning how she will write. *Lives of Girls and Women* remains to be written, and Del takes us back to her younger incarnation, sitting with Bobby Sherriff, to show us Del's opening response, at the beginning of her career as a writer, at the first end of our career as readers of this text. Presumably, Del will return to Bobby Sherriff's gesture through language, through writing things down, because the "only special thing" he ever does for her appears to Del to have a "concise meaning, a stylized meaning" which is written, performed in an "alphabet" she cannot read (211).

Del's closing gestures, like Bobby's, invite at least two readings. His wishing her luck in her life is a sincere and conventional gesture, to which Del might have responded with the expected "thank you."

But Del's actual response is more resonant, given that Bobby has just risen on his toes for her, in the last theatrical act in the novel. Del's "Yes" may well be the bold affirmation that we expect from a narrator who takes people's "wishes, and their other offerings," as if they were her due — "naturally, a bit distractedly" (211). But it may also be an acknowledgement of what she does not know, what she has just seen in Bobby's gesture — another entrance into the deep caves paved over with kitchen linoleum that are people's lives. "Thank you" would diminish Del's vocabulary, close her novel, and return us to the world. "Yes" opens out the possibilities of her imagination, affirms the powers of her fiction, and returns us to *Lives of Girls and Women*.

EPILOGUE: THE READER, THE TEXT, AND THE REAL

Any reading of a text is partial. It will vary with the varying circumstances of each reader's cultural experience, including its historical, national and regional, social and psychological dimensions. And a text like *Lives of Girls and Women*, with what I have read as its complementary forms, its invitations to contemplate mysteries, and its narrative intricacies, seems to multiply readings rather than consolidate them; I have read this tendency as a good thing. No reading is complete; any hope for such total authority is as "crazy, heartbreaking" as Del's hope for a total recapturing of her past, and probably a more serious delusion. And just as there are no total readings, it may be that there are no "true" readings; perhaps there are only "real" readings.

But if that were so, it would leave us with an obvious question: what is a "real" reading? This returns us to one of the central concerns of *Lives of Girls and Women*, and brings me to my conclusion by way of an essay of Munro's, "What Is Real?"

In the opening of her essay, Munro comments on the inevitable questions that arise when she is asked about her fiction:

"Do you write about real people?"
"Did those things really happen?"
"When you write about a small town are you really writing about Wingham?" (*Making It New* 223)

These are questions that relate directly to one of the tendencies we noted at the beginning of this study — to read *Lives of Girls and Women* as autobiography. Munro suggests that "people go on asking these same questions because the subject really does interest and bewilder them. It would seem to be quite true that they don't know what fiction is" (223). *Lives of Girls and Women* may help us to refine our ideas of how we read fiction by dissolving, just as Del dissolves, any hard and fast distinctions we might want to draw between fiction and reality, or between fiction and autobiography, between a life story and a life. Novels do not stand in direct opposition to reality; they do not present mirror images of reality; they do not explain reality. There are autobiographical elements in *Lives of Girls and Women*, as Munro has freely admitted; and there are ways in which Jubilee resembles Wingham. But fiction does not draw on what is real in any straightforward way; rather, fiction may be a kind of inquiry into what is real, an exploration of what is. But beyond any such investigative purpose, fiction also *creates* reality, performs a kind of reality. And reading fiction requires the same kind of creation and performance.

Del Jordan's explorations of what is real are readings, constructions of the experiences she recalls and reshapes into a novel, so that her life becomes a story — not a true story, but a real one. Del's story traces and enacts her development as a person and as a writer, developments that are intimately connected with her growth as a reader. Our readings of *Lives of Girls and Women* may not be true, but if they encourage us to rediscover the texts of the book, the world, and ourselves, they are real.

NOTES

1 See Munro's comments at the opening of "What Is Real?"
2 *Lives of Girls and Women*, p. 146, Signet reprint. All further references appear parenthetically in the text.
3 For an annotated selection of reviews of *Lives of Girls and Women*, see Robert Thacker's "Alice Munro: An Annotated Bibliography."
4 See, for example, Munro's comments in her interviews with John Metcalf and J.R. (Tim) Struthers.
5 See "Works Cited" for books by Dahlie, Pfaus, Martin, Blodgett, and Rasporich, and collections of essays edited by MacKendrick and Miller.

6 Thacker's bibliography is comprehensive in its listings of articles and parts of books on Munro's works appearing until June 30, 1982.
7 I am indebted to Carlene Besner for this insight.
8 In Gerson interview (4) and in Gibson interview (258).
9 For a discussion of the ways in which Munro's characters imagine the meanings of words, see Taylor's essay, "The Unimaginable Vancouvers: Alice Munro's Words."
10 For a thorough discussion of the texts that Del reads and how they educate her, see Blodgett, *Alice Munro*, chapter 3, "The Trope of Alpha" (37–60).
11 See, for example, J.R. (Tim) Struthers's essay, "Reality and Ordering: The Growth of a Young Artist in *Lives of Girls and Women*."
12 See "Walker Brothers Cowboy" in *Dance of the Happy Shades* (1968) for the finest example of a Munro story in which a father teaches his daughter, explicitly and implicitly, about several different versions of the past.
13 For an extended discussion of the transformations Del works through language in this scene, see Barbara Godard's essay, " 'Heirs of the Living Body': Alice Munro and the Question of a Female Aesthetic."
14 Compare Dunstan Ramsay's description in *Fifth Business* of the Deptford churches:

> We had five churches: the Anglican, poor but believed to have some mysterious social supremacy; the Presbyterian, solvent and thought — chiefly by itself — to be intellectual; the Methodist, insolvent and fervent; the Baptist, insolvent and saved; the Roman Catholic, mysterious to most of us but clearly solvent, as it was frequently and, so we thought, quite needlessly repainted. (10–11)

15 For an admirable discussion of the ways in which this chapter traces Del's search for the language of sexuality, see E.D. Blodgett, *Alice Munro*, 48–50.
16 *A Portrait of the Artist as a Young Man*, 247.
17 See Struthers, "Reality and Ordering," 45.
18 For a detailed discussion of this scene, see Smaro Kamboureli's essay, "The body as audience and performance in the writing of Alice Munro," 36.
19 See Struthers interview, 25.
20 See, for example, Juliann E. Fleenor's and Smaro Kamboureli's essays.
21 For an enumeration and detailed description of the Munro papers at the University of Calgary, see the *The Alice Munro Papers* (First and Second Accessions), ed. A. Steele.
22 See Polk, C. Thomas, and Johnson reviews, Struthers interview, Tausky essay, for example.

Works Cited

Agee, James, and Walker Evans. *Let Us Now Praise Famous Men*. Boston: Houghton, 1960.
Atwood, Margaret. *Survival: A Thematic Guide to Canadian Literature*. Toronto: Anansi, 1972.
Bailey, Nancy. "The Masculine Image in Lives of Girls and Women." *Canadian Literature* 80 (1979): 113-20.
  Examines the roles and images of men in the novel from a Jungian viewpoint.
Beers, Patricia. "Beside the Wawanash." Rev. of *Lives of Girls and Women*. *Times Literary Supplement* 17 Mar. 1978: 302.
Blodgett, E.D. *Alice Munro*. Twayne's World Authors Series 800. Boston: Twayne, 1988.
  The most thorough treatment of *Lives of Girls and Women* to date. Shows how Del reads various kinds of texts to discover what is real. Provides an annotated bibliography of selected secondary sources.
Bowen, Deborah. "In Camera: The Developed Photographs of Margaret Laurence and Alice Munro." *Studies in Canadian Literature* 13.1 (1988): 21-33.
  Considers photography in *The Diviners* and in *Lives of Girls and Women* as "the ground of her fiction making" for each writer. Draws on Barthes's and Sontag's discussions of photography.
Carscallen, James. "Alice Munro." *Profiles in Canadian Literature 2*. Ed. Jeffrey M. Heath. Toronto: Dundurn, 1980. 73-80.
  Introduces Munro as a short story writer and as a writer of *Bildungsromane*, novels about a young person's formation. Pays particular attention to *Lives of Girls and Women* and the structures of its stories.
Dahlie, Hallvard. *Alice Munro and Her Works*. Downsview, ON: ECW, 1985.
Davies, Robertson. *Fifth Business*. Toronto: Macmillan; New York: Viking, 1970. Penguin, 1977.
Davey, Frank. *From There to Here: A Guide to English-Canadian Literature Since 1960*. Our Nature — Our Voices 2. Erin, ON: Porcépic, 1974. 201-04.
Dawson, Anthony B. "Coming of Age in Canada." *Mosaic* 3 (1978): 47-62.
  Explores Del's growth as a person and writer in the context of other such Canadian stories, including works by Sinclair Ross, Laurence, W.O. Mitchell,

and Buckler. Sees major tension in book between Del's desire for "transcendence" and "sexual awakening and desire."

Daziron, Heliane. "Alice Munro's 'The Flats Road.'" *Canadian Woman Studies* 6.1 (1984): 103–04.

Argues that Munro's eccentrics in "The Flats Road" exert their influence in archetypal patterns. Draws on biblical figure of Jonah and of the ogress from folklore to discuss Uncle Benny and Madeleine.

Djwa, Sandra. "Deep Caves and Kitchen Linoleum: Psychological Violence in the Fiction of Alice Munro." *Violence in the Canadian Novel Since 1960 / Dans le Roman Canadien Depuis 1960.* Ed. Virginia Harger-Grinling and Terry Goldie. St. John's, NF: Memorial UP, 1981.

Fleenor, Juliann E. "Rape Fantasies as Initiation Rite: Female Imagination in *Lives of Girls and Women*." *Room of One's Own* 4.4 (1979): 35–49.

Argues that Del's "rape fantasy is the underlying structure of the novel, existing under the linear narrative, and it is through the rape fantasy that Del survives as a whole person and as an artist" (36).

Gerson, Carole. "Who Do You Think You Are?: Review-Interview with Alice Munro." *Room of One's Own* 4.4 (1979): 2–7.

Gibson, Graeme. "Alice Munro." *Eleven Canadian Novelists Interviewed by Graeme Gibson.* Toronto: Anansi, 1973. 239–64.

Godard, Barbara. " 'Heirs of the Living Body': Alice Munro and the Question of a Female Aesthetic." *The Art of Alice Munro: Saying the Unsayable.* Ed. Judith Miller. Waterloo: U of Waterloo P, 1984. 43–72.

Examines the ways in which Del's sexual awareness is also a textual awareness. Pays detailed attention to Del's glorying in the sounds and transformations of words as part of a "female aesthetic."

Hoy, Helen. " 'Dull, Simple, Amazing, and Unfathomable': Paradox and Double Vision in Alice Munro's Fiction." *Studies in Canadian Literature* 5.1 (1980): 100–15.

Shows how Munro's vision is reflected at the level of language and style, particularly through Munro's uses of pairs of adjectives that are contradictory to modify the same noun.

Hutcheon, Linda. *The Canadian Postmodern: A Survey of Contemporary English-Canadian Fiction.* Toronto: Oxford UP, 1988.

Irvine, Lorna. " 'Changing Is the Word I Want.' " MacKendrick 99–111.

Shows how transformation and ambiguity are essential female attributes in Munro's fiction, reflecting women's experience.

Joyce, James. *A Portrait of the Artist as a Young Man.* New York: Viking, 1956.

Jackson, Heather. Rev. of *Lives of Girls and Women*. *The Canadian Forum* Jan.–Feb. 1972: 76–77.

Johnson, Marigold. "Mud and Blood." Rev. of *Lives of Girls and Women*. *New Statesman* 26 Oct. 1973: 619.

Kamboureli, Smaro. "The body as audience and performance in the writing of

Alice Munro." *A Mazing Space: Writing Canadian Women Writing*. Ed. Shirley Neuman and Smaro Kamboureli. Edmonton: Longspoon and NeWest, 1986. 31–39.

Studies the ways in which women's bodies and experiences are represented or inscribed in the text. Closely analyzes Del's language from feminist perspectives.

Keith, W.J. *Canadian Literature in English*. White Plains, NY: Longman's, 1985.

Kröller, Eva-Marie. "The Eye in the Text: Timothy Findley's *The Last of the Crazy People* and Alice Munro's *Lives of Girls and Women*." *World Literature Written in English* 23.2 (1984): 366–74.

Shows how various forms of seeing operate in both novels to undermine the apparently realistic surface narratives. Suggests that readers are invited to engage in a similar process and progress to the protagonists' "visual/sexual initiation."

Laurence, Margaret. *A Bird in the House*. Toronto: McClelland; New York: Knopf; London: Macmillan, 1970.

MacKendrick, Louis, ed. *Probable Fictions: Alice Munro's Narrative Acts*. Downsview, ON: ECW, 1983.

Martin, W.R. *Alice Munro: Paradox and Parallel*. Edmonton: U of Alberta P, 1987.

———. "The Strange and Familiar in Alice Munro." *Studies in Canadian Literature* 7 (1982): 214–26.

———. "Alice Munro and James Joyce." *Journal of Canadian Fiction* 24 (1979): 120–26.

McCarthy MacDonald, Rae. "Structure and Detail in Lives of Girls and Women." *Studies in Canadian Literature* 3 (1988): 199–210.

Explores the ways in which the details of everyday life function in relation to the crises of Del's struggles between the demands of two realities — "the world" and the "other country." Argues that Del's crises are finally less important than the ways in which daily life undermines her.

McMullen, Lorraine. " 'Shameless, Marvellous, Shattering Absurdity': The Humour of Paradox in Alice Munro." MacKendrick 144–62.

Shows how Munro uses paradox to reveal ambiguity, particularly through her uses of paradox in her narrators' language.

McPherson, Hugo. "Fiction 1940–1960." *Literary History of Canada: Canadian Literature in English*. Gen. ed. Carl F. Klinck. Toronto: U of Toronto P, 1965.

Metcalf, John. "A Conversation with Alice Munro." *Journal of Canadian Fiction* 1.4 (1972): 54–62.

Miller, Judith, ed. *The Art of Alice Munro: Saying the Unsayable*. Waterloo: U of Waterloo P, 1984.

Moss, John. "Alice in the Looking Glass: Munro's *Lives of Girls and Women*." *Sex and Violence in the Canadian Novel: The Ancestral Present*. Toronto: McClelland, 1977.

_____. *A Reader's Guide to the Canadian Novel.* Second ed.; First ed. 1981. Toronto: McClelland, 1987.

Munro, Alice. *Dance of the Happy Shades.* Toronto: Ryerson, 1968.

_____. *Lives of Girls and Women.* Toronto: McGraw-Hill Ryerson, 1971. Scarborough, ON: Signet, 1974.

_____. *Something I've Been Meaning to Tell You: Thirteen Stories.* Toronto: McGraw-Hill Ryerson; New York: McGraw-Hill, 1974.

_____. *Who Do You Think You Are?* Toronto: Macmillan, 1978.

_____. *The Moons of Jupiter.* Toronto: Macmillan, 1982.

_____. "What Is Real?" *The Canadian Forum* Sept. 1982: 5, 36. Rpt. in *Making It New: Contemporary Canadian Stories.* Ed. John Metcalf. Toronto: Methuen, 1982. 223–26.

_____. *The Progress of Love.* Toronto: McClelland; New York: Knopf, 1986.

_____. *Friend of My Youth.* Toronto: McClelland; New York: Knopf, 1990.

New, William H. "Fiction." *Literary History of Canada: Canadian Literature in English.* Gen. ed. and introd. Carl F. Klinck. 2nd ed. Toronto: U of Toronto P, 1976. 3: 233–83

_____. *A History of Canadian Literature.* Macmillan History of Literature. Gen. ed. A. Norman Jeffares. London: Macmillan, 1989.

Orange, John. "Alice Munro and A Maze of Time." MacKendrick 83–93.

Packer, Miriam. "*Lives of Girls and Women*: A Creative Search for Completion." *The Canadian Novel: Here and Now.* Ed. John Moss. Toronto: NC, 1978. 1: 134–44.

Studies Del's personal and artistic growth, showing how each of the eight chapters records a stage of Del's development. Suggests that all of these developments are incomplete and tentative.

Pfaus, B. *Alice Munro.* Ottawa: Golden Dog, 1984.

Polk, James. "Deep Caves and Kitchen Linoleum." Rev. of *Lives of Girls and Women. Canadian Literature* 54 (1972): 102–04.

Sees the novel's chapters as "basically unpruned short stories," but praises the book for its depiction of Ontario small-town life and for its success in using the conventional patterns of first novels.

Rasporich, Beverly. *The Dance of the Sexes: Art and Gender in the Fiction of Alice Munro.* Edmonton: U of Alberta P, 1989.

Robson, Nora. "Alice Munro and the White American South: The Quest." *The Art of Alice Munro: Saying the Unsayable.* Ed. Judith Miller. Waterloo: U of Waterloo P, 1984. 73–84.

Rudzik, O.H.T. Rev. of *Lives of Girls and Women.* "Letters in Canada: Fiction." *University of Toronto Quarterly* 41 (1972): 308–18.

Rule, Jane. "The Credible Woman." Rev. of *Lives of Girls and Women. Books in Canada* Nov. 1971: 4–5.

Points out that Del's story is about the development of an artist as well as the growth of a person.

Stephens, Donald. "Bright New Day." *Canadian Literature* 54 (1972): 84–86.
Steele, Apollonia, and Jean F. Tener, eds., and Jean F. Moore and Jean F. Tener, comps. *The Alice Munro Papers: First Accession: An Inventory of the Archive at the University of Calgary Libraries.* Calgary: Calgary UP, 1986.
Steele, Apollonia, and Jean F. Tener, eds., and Jean F. Moore, comp. *The Alice Munro Papers: Second Accession: An Inventory of the Archive at the University of Calgary Libraries.* Calgary: Calgary UP, 1987.
Steele, Charles. *Taking Stock: The Calgary Conference on the Canadian Novel.* Downsview, ON: ECW, 1982.
Story, Norah. *The Oxford Companion to Canadian History and Literature.* Toronto: Oxford UP, 1967.
Struthers, J.R. (Tim). "The Real Material: An Interview with Alice Munro." MacKendrick 5–36.
A wide-ranging conversation about Munro's fiction, with an important discussion of the genesis of *Lives of Girls and Women.*
———. "Reality and Ordering: The Growth of a Young Artist in *Lives of Girls and Women.*" *Essays on Canadian Writing* 3 (1975): 32–46.
Argues that *Lives of Girls and Women* is a künstlerroman, the story of the development of an artist, and shows parallels and connections between Munro's novel and Joyce's fiction, particularly *A Portrait of the Artist as a Young Man.*
———. "Alice Munro and the American South." *Canadian Review of American Studies* 6 (1975): 196–204; rev. and rpt. in *The Canadian Novel: Here and Now.* Ed. John Moss. Toronto: NC, 1978. 1: 121–33.
———. "Some Highly Subversive Activities: A Brief Polemic and a Checklist of Works on Alice Munro." *Studies in Canadian Literature* 6 (1981): 140–50.
———. "Short Fiction in English." *The Canadian Encyclopedia.* 1985, rev. ed. 1988.
Tausky, Thomas E. " 'What Happened to Marion?': Art and Reality in *Lives of Girls and Women.*" *Studies in Canadian Literature* 11.1 (1986): 52–76.
Studies "Epilogue: The Photographer," drawing on earlier drafts collected in Alice Munro papers at the University or Calgary, and on conversations with Munro, to discuss how Del's unwritten novel reflects her (and Munro's) vision of writing.
Taylor, Michael. "The Unimaginable Vancouvers: Alice Munro's Words." MacKendrick 127–43.
Traces Munro's recurrent exploration of words in her fiction.
Thacker, Robert. "Alice Munro: An Annotated Bibliography." *The Annotated Bibliography of Canada's Major Authors.* Ed. Robert Lecker and Jack David. Downsview, ON: ECW, 1984. 5: 354–414
Lists Munro's works and provides detailed summaries of works about Munro, including articles, parts of books, audio-visual material, theses and dissertations, interviews, and book reviews.

———. " 'Clear Jelly': Alice Munro's Narrative Dialectics." MacKendrick 127–43.

———. " 'So Shocking a Verdict in Real Life': Autobiography in Alice Munro's Stories." *Reflections: Autobiography and Canadian Literature.* Ed. K.P. Stich. Ottawa: U of Ottawa P, 1988. 153–62.

Argues that autobiography informs much of Munro's fiction, which, like autobiography, takes as its central task the "definition of self."

Thomas, Clara. "Woman Invincible." Rev. of *Lives of Girls and Women. Journal of Canadian Fiction* 1.4 (1972): 95–96.

Traces Del Jordan's fictional lineage to L.M. Montgomery's *Anne of Green Gables*, comments on Del Jordan's power, and discusses the purpose of "Epilogue: The Photographer."

Wallace, Bronwen. "Women's Lives: Alice Munro." *The Human Elements.* Ed. David Helwig. Ottawa: Oberon, 1978. 52–67.

Shows from a feminist perspective how Munro's fiction explores the whole range of women's experience.

Warwick, Susan J. "Growing Up: The Novels of Alice Munro." *Essays on Canadian Writing* 29 (1984): 204–25.

Compares the narrative technique of *Lives of Girls and Women* with that of *Who Do You Think You Are?*, showing how narration functions to convey our sense of Del's and Rose's development.

Waterston, Elizabeth. *Survey: A Short History of Canadian Literature.* Toronto: Methuen, 1973.

Wayne, Joyce. "Huron County Blues." *Books in Canada* Oct. 1982: 9–12.

Provides biographical information on Munro, including Wingham's reactions to Munro's fiction.

Weaver, Robert. "Short Stories in English." *The Oxford Companion to Canadian Literature.* Ed. William Toye. Toronto: Oxford UP, 1983.

Welty, Eudora. *The Golden Apples.* New York: Harcourt, 1949.

Wolff, Geoffrey. "Call It Fiction." Rev. of *Lives of Girls and Women. Time* 15 Jan. 1973: 79.

Wordsworth, Christopher. "Maple Leaf in Bud." Rev. of *Lives of Girls and Women. Manchester Guardian Weekly* 3 Nov. 1973: 24.

York, Lorraine M. "Lives of Joan and Del: Separate Paths to Transformation in *Lives of Girls and Women* and *Lady Oracle*." *University of Windsor Review* 19.2 (1986): 1–10.

Shows how Joan's and Del's paths towards personal and artistic freedom are "separate but parallel," noting both characters' discarding of the image of the Tennysonian heroine.

———. *"The Other Side of Dailiness": Photography in the Works of Alice Munro, Timothy Findley, Michael Ondaatje, and Margaret Laurence.* Toronto: ECW, 1987.

Index

"Age of Faith" (Munro) 32, 62–68
Agee, James 29
Alice Munro (Blodgett) 25, 28, 31
"Alice Munro and the American South" (Struthers) 27, 29
"Alice Munro: An Annotated Bibliography" (Thacker) 25
"Alice Munro and James Joyce" (Martin) 26
"Alice in the Looking Glass: *Lives of Girls and Women*" (Moss) 18
"Alice Munro and a Maze of Time" (Orange) 28
Alice Munro: Paradox and Parallel (Martin) 25, 27
"Alice Munro and the White American South: The Quest" (Robson) 27
Alther, Lisa 22
Anne of Green Gables (Montgomery) 23
Atwood, Margaret 17
Aunt Elspeth (character) 44–46, 49–50
Auntie Grace (character) 44–46, 49–50

"Baptizing" (Munro) 66, 85, 89–103
Beers, Patricia 22
Bird in the House, A (Laurence) 14
Blodgett, E.D. 25, 28, 31
"Body as Audience and Performance in the Writing of Alice Munro, The" (Kamboureli) 30
Books in Canada 22

Bowen, Deborah 29
"Bright New Day, The" (Stephens) 19

Canadian Encyclopedia, The 20
Canadian Forum, The 22
Canadian Literature (periodical) 18–19, 23
Canadian Literature in English (Keith) 18
Canadian Postmodern, The: A Survey of Contemporary English-Canadian Fiction (Hutcheon) 18
Caroline (character) 106–09
Chamberlain, Art (character) 78–89
"Changes and Ceremonies" (Munro) 69–78, 93
"Changing Is the Word I Want" (Irvine) 30
" 'Clear Jelly': Alice Munro's Narrative Dialectics" (Thacker) 27
Clive (character) 91–92

Danby, Ken 29
Dance of the Happy Shades (Munro) 17, 92
Davey, Frank 17
Davies, Robertson 65
"Deep Caves and Kitchen Linoleum" (Polk) 23–24
"Deep Caves and Kitchen Linoleum: Psychological Violence in the Fiction of Alice Munro" (Djwa) 27

Del's grandmother (character) 58–59, 61
Djwa, Sandra 27
Dogherty, Fern (character) 78–79, 81–82
"'Dull, Simple, Amazing, and Unfathomable': Paradox and Double Vision in Alice Munro's Fiction" (Hoy) 26–27

"Epilogue: The Photographer" (Munro) 23, 24, 29, 59, 103–12
Evans, Walker 29

Farris, Miss (character) 73–78
Fifth Business (Davies) 65
"Flats Road, The" (Munro) 35–42, 100
Fleenor, Juliann E. 30
French, Garnet (character) 66, 95–103
From There to Here: A Guide to English-Canadian Literature Since 1960 (Davey) 17

Gallant, Mavis 19
Godard, Barbara 30
Golden Apples, The (Welty) 27
"Growing Up: The Novels of Alice Munro" (Warwick) 28

"Heirs of the Living Body" (Munro) 42–50, 111
"'Heirs of the Living Body': Alice Munro and the Question of a Female Aesthetic" (Godard) 30
History of Canadian Literature, A (New) 18
Hoy, Helen 26–27, 56
Hutcheon, Linda 18

"In Camera: The Developed Photographs of Margaret Laurence and Alice Munro" (Bowen) 29
Irvine, Lorna 30

Jackson, Heather 22
Johnson, Marigold 21
Jordan, Del (character) 12–15, 31, 32–50, 52–62, 64–104, 106–13
Journal of Canadian Fiction 22–23
Joyce, James 26, 39
Jubilee 12, 36, 37, 41, 46, 55–56, 64, 65, 90, 94, 100, 107, 110, 113

Kamboureli, Smaro 30
Keith, W.J. 18
Kinflicks (Alther) 22
Künstlerroman 14, 26

Lady Oracle (Atwood) 26
Laurence, Margaret 14, 29
Let Us Now Praise Famous Men (Agee and Evans) 29
Literary History of Canada, The: Canadian Literature in English (McPherson) 17
"Lives of Girls and Women" (Munro) 78–89
"*Lives of Girls and Women*: A Creative Search for Completion" (Packer) 26
"Lives of Joan and Del: Separate Paths to Transformation in *Lives of Girls and Women* and *Lady Oracle*" (York) 26

Madeleine (character) 39–40
Manchester Guardian Weekly, The 20
"Maple Leaf in Bud" (Wordsworth) 20
Martin, W.R. 25, 26, 27
McPherson, Hugo 17
Metcalf, John 32, 35
Montgomery, L.M. 23
Morrison, Addie (character) 14, 41, 43, 46, 49, 50, 52–62, 78, 79–80, 90
Moss, John 18

Naomi (character) 72–73, 92
New, William 17, 18

New Statesman 21

Oliphant, Mary Agnes (character) 43, 47
Orange, John 28
Other Side of Dailiness, The: Photography in the Works of Alice Munro, Timothy Findley, Michael Ondaatje, and Margaret Laurence (York) 29
"Ottawa Valley, The" (Munro) 30
"Ounce of Cure, An" (Munro) 90
Owen (character) 13, 33, 54, 57, 66, 68
Oxford Companion to Canadian Literature, The 20

Packer, Miriam 26
"Paralyzed Artist, The" (Atwood) 17
Phippen, Bella (character) 71
Polk, James 19, 23–25
Portrait of the Artist as a Young Man, A (Joyce) 26, 39
"Princess Ida" (Munro) 50–62

RANAM (Recherches Anglaises et Nord-Americaines) 20
"Rape Fantasies and Initiation Rites: Female Imagination in *Lives of Girls and Women*" (Fleenor) 30
Reader's Guide to the Canadian Novel, A (Moss) 18
"Real Material, The: An Interview with Alice Munro" (Struthers) 32
"Reality and Ordering: The Growth of a Young Artist in *Lives of Girls and Women*" (Struthers) 26
Robson, Nora (27)
Rudzik, O.H.T. 22
Rule, Jane 22

Sex and Violence in the Canadian Novel: The Ancestral Present (Moss) 18
Sherriff, Bobby (character) 109, 111–12

Sherriff, Marion (character) 106–10
"Short Fiction in English" (Struthers) 20
"Short Stories in English" (Weaver) 20
" 'So Shocking a Verdict in Real Life' ": Autobiography in Alice Munro's Stories" (Thacker) 28
Steele, Charles 18
Stephens, Donald 19
Storey, Jerry (character) 92–95, 97–98
Story, Norah 17
"Strange and Familiar in Alice Munro, The" (Martin) 27
Struthers, J.R. (Tim) 20, 25, 26, 27, 29, 32, 89
Studies in Canadian Literature 25
"Sunbather, The" (Danby) 29
Supplement to the Oxford Companion to Canadian History and Literature 17
Survey: A Short History of Canadian Literature (Waterston) 17
Survival: A Thematic Guide to Canadian Literature (Atwood) 17

Taking Stock: The Calgary Conference on the Canadian Novel (Steele) 18
Tausky, Thomas 103
Thacker, Robert 25, 28
Thomas, Clara 22–23
Time 21
Times Literary Supplement, The 22

Ulysses (Joyce) 25
Uncle Benny (character) 35–41
Uncle Bill (character) 59–61
Uncle Craig (character) 42–44, 111
University of Toronto Quarterly 22

Wales, Frank (character) 74–76, 93
Wallace, Bronwen 30
Warwick, Susan 28
Waterston, Elizabeth 17

Wawanash River 76–77, 100
Weaver, Robert 20
Welty, Eudora 27
" 'What Happened to Marion?': Art and Reality in *Lives of Girls and Women*" (Tausky) 103
"What Is Real?" (Munro) 112
Who Do You Think You Are? (Munro) 28, 29, 92
Wolff, Geoffrey 21
"Women's Lives: Alice Munro" (Wallace) 30
Woodcock, George 18
Wordsworth, Christopher 20
World Literature Written in English 19

York, Lorraine M. 26, 29